History of

Savings and Loan in Texas

RESEARCH MONOGRAPH NUMBER SEVENTEEN

History of

Savings and Loan in Texas

by JACK W. CASHIN

Assistant Professor of Finance, College of Business Administration
The University of Texas

Published for the
Texas Savings and Loan League

BUREAU OF BUSINESS RESEARCH
College of Business Administration, The University of Texas
Austin, 1956

Printed and bound in Austin by The University of Texas Printing Division

History of

SAVINGS AND LOAN
IN TEXAS

by

JACK W. CASHIN

Savings and loan activity is big business in Texas. Already past the billion-dollar mark, this industry plays a major part in the financial life of the state.

Never before, however, has a comprehensive study of the growth of savings and loan in Texas been made. Dr. Cashin draws together detailed information heretofore unavailable in any single book and analyzes the striking growth pattern of the entire industry

After discussing the beginnings of the savings and loan movement in England and America, Dr. Cashin tells how Texas savings and loan activity began in 1866 with the Young Men's Mutual Real Estate and Building Association. He follows the frequently stormy growth of the industry from the Reconstruction Period following the Civil War through the post-World War II boom years.

This book, richly documented, is a major contribution to the historical records of Texas. More important, it is the living story of the development of an important American business institution, the savings and loan association.

Jack W. Cashin inaugurated, in 1955, the first college course in the United States devoted entirely to the savings and loan industry. As a member of the faculty of the College of Business Administration at The University of Texas, Dr. Cashin has carried on intensive research in Texas financial institutions. Originally from New York State, the author is a Texan by choice and has taught at The University of Texas since 1950. He is a member of the Phi Beta Kappa and Beta Gamma Sigma honorary fraternities.

Foreword

History of Savings and Loan in Texas is the seventeenth publication to be included in the monograph series of the Bureau of Business Research. The study is an adaptation of one submitted by Dr. Cashin to the Faculty of the Graduate School of The University of Texas as partial fulfillment of the requirements for the degree of Doctor of Philosophy. The Bureau has long been interested in all phases of Texas business, and the staff believes that Dr. Cashin's survey will do much to further public knowledge of savings and loan, a vital segment of the Texas economy.

A generous grant from the Texas Savings and Loan League enabled the Bureau to undertake publication of the study. Editorial work on the monograph was handled by Robert H. Ryan with the assistance of James H. Keahey and Roberta Steele.

STANLEY A. ARBINGAST
Assistant Director

Preface

The savings and loan industry in Texas occupies a prominent position among the financial activities of the state. At the close of 1955, Texas savings and loan associations had assets in excess of $1 billion. Because of the nature of the industry, changes in savings and loan activity often reflect other economic changes within the state. The writer became interested in savings and loan associations while, as an instructor at The University of Texas, he had occasion to study Texas financial institutions.

A grant from the Texas Savings and Loan League to the Department of Finance, Insurance, and Real Estate to encourage teaching in the field of savings and loan associations made the publication of this book possible. While space is too limited to mention all of those in the savings and loan industry who have assisted during the preparation of this book, the author must acknowledge the contribution made by the Education Committee of the Texas Savings and Loan League. ,The Education Committee includes: Mr. Alton J. Luckett, Chairman, New Braunfels; Mr. Gus L. Berry, Dallas; Mr. Lloyd S. Bowles, Dallas; Mr. A. H. Knippa, San Antonio; Mr. Charles W. Cart, San Antonio; and Mr. William G. Richards, Houston. Both Mr. Berry and Mr. Luckett read the complete manuscript and made valuable suggestions. Mr. Luckett followed the book through the many stages of publication and gave much assistance along the way.

Dr. Charles L. Prather, Professor of Finance at The University of Texas, guided the preparation of this study with wisdom born of his long experience in the field of financial research. Dr. E. Karl McGinnis, also of The University of Texas business administration faculty, made many helpful contributions, particularly in regard to the sections dealing with the recent progress of savings and loan activity in Texas.

Mr. Ray A. Benson, Savings, Building and Loan Supervisor of the State of Texas; Mr. Walter W. McAllister, Chairman of the Federal Home Loan Bank Board; Mr. J. Curran Conway, President of the Federal Home Loan Bank of Little Rock; and Mr. Charles M. Torrance, Director, Operating Analysis Division, Federal Savings and Loan Insurance Corporation, provided the writer with important information which would otherwise have been unavailable to him.

Finally, the author wishes to express his gratitude to his wife, Mrs. Margaret Mary Thorpe Cashin, for her encouragement and assistance during the preparation of this work.

March 1956.   J. W. C.

Table of Contents

List of Tables

List of Maps

CHAPTER I

Introduction

THE SAVINGS and loan industry in Texas constitutes an important segment of the financial activity of the state. Texas has no mutual savings banks, but there are commercial banks and other financial institutions which do compete directly with savings and loan associations in the savings and urban mortgage lending field.

Though a latecomer to Texas, the savings and loan industry is vigorous and fast growing. Over the last twenty years, total assets owned by Texas associations have increased from approximately $70 million in 1935 to over $1 billion in 1955. Because of the nature of its activities, the savings and loan industry is closely linked with new construction, urbanization, industrialization, and various other aspects of the rapid growth of Texas.

Not only has the savings and loan industry in Texas grown in size; it has also grown in complexity. Typical associations have changed from small concerns which acted essentially as real estate loan companies to large financial institutions able to cope with the many and varied financial needs of a modern, complex economic system.

The two main functions of a savings and loan association are accepting savings and making urban real estate loans. Thus, the industry accepts as its goal the dual functions of encouraging thrift and promoting home ownership. By most standards these are desirable ends, and it is largely in terms of ways and means of better reaching these goals that the history of the industry unfolds. Though few would quarrel with the desirability of the goals, there have been, throughout the history of savings and loan activity in Texas, repeated disputes as to the means whereby these ends could best be achieved. The path of development has been difficult, at times almost impossible, and it makes interesting reading.

This book is the story of the savings and loan movement in Texas and as such, the primary purpose has been to chronicle the developments and changes within the industry as well as other developments which have either supplemented or encouraged its development. In a broad sense, there is scarcely a segment of economic activity which has not in some manner affected savings and loan development. However, this book has necessarily been restricted to the history of the industry and the other factors that have most directly influenced its development.

The savings and loan industry is so closely tied to the public that both

I

state and federal governments have subjected it to close scrutiny. As a consequence, the legal rules under which savings and loan associations operate are closely defined. To a large extent, an understanding of savings and loan operation presupposes an understanding of the many pertinent laws.

The reader will find much of the material contained in this book to have come from sources not generally available to the reading public. For this reason, it may also serve as a reference or source book for statistical and other information.

An attempt has been made in this book to avoid the use of terms and words which would require definition or explanation. In the few instances where it has been necessary to employ a term in a technical sense with a meaning different from its usual one, it has been defined at the point of first use. This was necessary in dealing with the various plans and forms of stock employed by savings and loan associations. It does seem desirable, however, to define the term "savings and loan association" as used herein. While there are many definitions of the term, the one used by Professor Charles L. Prather was selected; this describes a savings and loan association as an institution "organized to make loans to home-owners and to conduct a savings business."[1] These associations have been known by a variety of names. In late years the title "savings and loan association" has been the most popular; for the first century of their existence the title "building and loan association" was the more common one. Associations have operated with titles of:

. . . Homestead and Building Associations, Mutual Loan Associations, Cooperative banks, Cooperative Saving and Loan Associations, Savings Fund and Loan Associations, Savings and Building Associations, Savings and Loan Companies, and other titles of like nature.[2]

At the present time there seems to be a growing trend toward dropping the "loan" and referring to them as simply "savings associations."

The title of the association may give a clue to the reason for which it was organized and, possibly, to its method of operation. Savings and loan associations do not accept deposits, as do commercial banks; instead they sell shares to investors. To this extent, savings and loan associations are mutual or member-owned institutions. All associations appeal to the thrift-minded investor by providing a place for his savings. For the most part, savings and loan associations invest their funds in mortgages incurred in the building or purchasing of homes. Though this is not a requirement, savings and loan

---

[1] Charles L. Prather, *Money and Banking* (5th ed.) (Homewood: Richard D. Irwin, Incorporated, 1953), p. 496.

[2] Henry S. Rosenthal, *Building, Loan and Savings Associations* (3rd ed.) (Cincinnati: American Building Association News Company, 1911), p. 4.

associations are thought of as institutions which lend predominantly on urban real estate.

The rapid growth of the savings and loan industry, though desirable, has created many problems that must be faced by the industry. For the most part, these are problems of personnel, for the industry has grown more rapidly than the supply of trained personnel to man it. This explains in part the high regard in which education is held by savings and loan people. Industry-sponsored schools, conferences, and seminars have been held for many years. In 1955 The University of Texas, the first school in the nation to do so, offered a regularly scheduled course in savings and loan. This was made possible by a grant by the Texas Savings and Loan League.

Traditionally the savings and loan industry has been associated with progress and development. Because of its nature, if an association operates effectively, it will follow activities which contribute to economic development. At first glance, the savings and loan movement will seem to contain many paradoxes and indeed it does. So far as investment of the public's funds is concerned associations do and must behave in a typically conservative manner. On the other hand, the amortized loan based in large measure on the salary of a working man was, at the time of its inception, a drastic departure from existing loan methods. As an industry, it is motivated by principles of private enterprise and resists government intervention; however, the industry itself has sought government supervision and control when it was found necessary to stamp out unscrupulous or fraudulent practices which tended to undermine the whole structure. The two goals of savings and loan activity, the promotion of thrift and of home ownership, at first appear to be mutually contradictory. A more thorough examination will reveal, however, that what first appeared to be a paradox has become an attempt to balance one goal against another in such a manner as to achieve a degree of both.

Historically the savings and loan movement in Texas has been closely linked with the economic development of the state. And there is every reason to believe that in the years ahead, the savings and loan industry will come to play an increasingly important role in the financial life of Texas.

CHAPTER II

The Savings and Loan Movement
in the United States

While the main purpose of this book is to present the history of savings and loan associations in Texas, it is necessary to trace early movements and developments in the United States; for the savings and loan associations which were organized in Texas, beginning in the late 1860's, were affected by the evolution and changes which had occurred within the industry.

The immediate ancestor of the American savings and loan association was the building society of England. The building society was part of the cooperative movement which swept Great Britain in the late seventeenth and early eighteenth centuries. The first such society in England was started in Birmingham in 1781.[1] This was followed by several other British associations or societies which have been described as:

The means whereby the industrial classes of Great Britain have supplied their economic needs for themselves, no man showing them the way, not by prescription nor by influence of superiors.[2]

The first savings and loan association to be formed in the United States was the Oxford Provident Association of Frankfort, Pennsylvania, organized in 1831. Frankfort, then an independent burough, has since become a part of Philadelphia.

Two influential manufacturers in Frankfort, Samuel Pilling and Jeremiah Horrocks, and one physician, Dr. Henry Taylor, had immigrated from England and were familiar with the building societies that had been in existence there since 1781. These three men believed that a building society would be of assistance in helping working people to help themselves. They enlisted the aid of Jesse Y. Castor, a local lawyer, and held a meeting on January 3, 1831, "at the inn of Thomas Sidebotham, at what is now 4219 Frankfort Avenue,"[3] for the purpose of organizing such an association.

The minute book which contains complete records of the association is now in the custody of the Historical Society of Frankfort.[4] The minutes

---

[1] H. Morton Bodfish (ed.), *History of Building and Loan in the United States* (Chicago: United States Building and Loan League, 1931), p. 11.
[2] *Ibid.*
[3] *Ibid.*, p. 35.
[4] *Ibid.*

show that the management of the association was assigned to thirteen trustees, who were to serve without compensation and were to operate the association for the purpose of enabling "the subscribers, most of whom were wage earners in the textile trade, to build or purchase dwelling houses."[5]

The par value of shares of the Oxford Provident Association was $500, and members were allowed to make initial payments of $5.00 and contribute $3.00 a month until their shares were paid for. No member was allowed to purchase more than five shares. A member was allowed to borrow $500 for each share he agreed to purchase, and loans were made to the members making the highest bids. The loans could only be made on real estate within five miles of Frankfort. The association was to continue in business until every member who desired to do so was able to purchase or build a home. It operated for a period of ten years and was dissolved in 1841.

Many of the provisions found in the Oxford Provident Association were to reappear in subsequent associations. The association was not organized with a view toward making a profit; instead, it was a cooperative venture with the humanitarian objective of assisting individuals to own their homes. This cooperative and altruistic motive was to prompt the organization of many later associations.[6]

The method of granting loans on the basis of the highest bid was to be used in some of the associations operating nearly a half-century later in Texas. The subscription to, and purchase of, shares of stock on the instalment plan still prevails to a limited degree. While the five-mile limitation referred to above no longer applies, savings and loan associations still restrict their operations, for the most part, to making loans on local urban real estate.

The first loan made by the Oxford Provident Association was to Mr. Comly Rich, who offered a premium of ten dollars. But Rich had difficulty making the payments and was often charged a late penalty. Finally the property was transferred to Mr. Duffield, apparently an amicable settlement of the account. Bodfish was able to find the house upon which the first loan was made; it was still standing and occupied in 1931.[7]

Because of its historic interest, the constitution of the Oxford Provident Association is reproduced on the following pages.[8]

[5] *Ibid.*

[6] In order to qualify as a cooperative, an association must meet the two following tests: (1) voting rights depend upon membership, not stock ownership; and (2) distribution of profits is on the basis of patronage and not ownership. When all members both save and borrow, and when all earnings eventually accrue to the members, this second requirement is automatically achieved.

[7] Now maintained as a monument to the beginning of the savings and loan movement.

[8] *Ibid.*, pp. 37–43.

January 3rd 1831

At a meeting of sundry inhabitants of the
Borough of Frankford and its vicinity held
this day pursuant to public notice at the
house of Thomas Sidebotham in said Borough
for the purpose of forming an association
to enable the contributors thereof to build
or purchase dwelling houses. Isaac Whitelock
was called to the chair and Jesse Y Castor
was appointed secretary.

On Motion and seconded the following Constitution
was unanimously adopted for the Government of
said association

Article 1st

This association shall be known by the name
style and title of the Oxford Provident Building
Association of Philadelphia County

Article 2nd

This Association shall be conducted by thirteen
Trustees who shall at the stated meetings in Janu
ary and July in each and every year elect a President,
from their own body and a secretary from amongst the
members and such other officers as the business of the
institution may require. The seat of any trustee who
shall be absent for three successive stated meetings
may be vacated by the Board at any stated meeting
thereof, and any officer by them appointed may be
removed at pleasure

Art 3rd

The trustees shall have power to fill up by
ballot after notice of one month any vacancy which
may happen in their body or officers not less than
two thirds of the whole Board to be present when any
appointment or removal is acted upon

Article 4th

The trustees shall not receive either directly, or indirectly any compensation for their services

Article 5th

The Treasurer shall be elected by ballot by the members at the semi annual meetings in January to serve one year whose duty it shall be to keep a just and true account, in a book or books to be kept for the purpose of all the monies paid him by the members either as fines or contributions. He shall have in charge and shall be responsible for all monies by him received from time to time and shall at the stated meeting in January and July in each and every year render to the society a correct statement of the fiscal concerns of the same or whenever required by the trustees

He shall attend every stated meeting of the association unless prevented by sickness or other unavoidable cause and for neglect of duty shall be fined by the president or in his absence by the President Pro tempore in any such sum as may be specified by the Bye laws

He shall give such security as the trustees shall deem sufficient for the faithful performance of his duties and for the payment of the balance due by him to the association and for the delivery of the books and papers belonging to the same to his successor in office

Art 6th

The trustees shall be elected by ballot at the stated meetings in January and July in each and every year the term of service of six of the Youngest trustees now elected shall expire at the next stated meeting in July and six others be elected to supply their places to serve for the ensuing year so that at the end of every six months the term of either seven or six trustees shall expire

No trustee shall be incapable of re election nor

shall he be obliged to serve more than one year
out of three

It shall be the duty of the trustees in addition to
those specified to cause all bills for lumber and materials to be paid through the Treasury where they consider the same just and fair and shall assign to the treas
urer and secretary or other officers for their services
such compensation as they shall think reasonable

Article 7th

The president shall preside at all meetings of the trustees
and association and shall preserve order and regulate debate
for the infraction whereof he shall impose such fines
as may be designated by the Bye laws

He shall sign all orders on the Treasurer for the pay
ment of money when directed so to do by the Building
committee

Article 8th

It shall be the duty of the secretary to keep fair min
utes of every Transaction of the trustees and of the asso
ciation. He shall keep a book or books containing a list of
the members with an account opened with each. He shall
have in charge all books and papers belonging to the associ
ation except those of the Treasurer and shall deliver the
same to his successor in office

Article 9th

Each member shall pay the sum of five dollars
upon each share of stock held by him and a month
ly contribution of three dollars on each and every share
by him held

Article 10th

The trustees shall from time to time as the funds
of the association will justify give notice at a stated
meeting that at the next stated meeting they will be
prepared to advance money to one or more members
as the case may be which shall not exceed the sum

of five hundred dollars on each share by him or them
held which said money so advanced shall be applyd
to the purpose of purchasing or building a dwelling
house or houses and no other. In every case the party or
parties desirous to borrow the said sum or sums or sum
of money shall at the stated meeting offer by a written
ballot with his name thereon specifying what premium
he or they are willing to give for the same and the member
or members offering the highest sum shall be entitled to the
same

Article 11th

When any member shall be declared to be entitled
to a loan or loans it will be his duty to inform the
Building committee of the trustees of his having pur
chased a house or houses or a lot to erect one or more
thereon the title papers for which shall be submitted
to them for inspection and if they are satisfied with
the same or any other collateral security which may
be offered they shall permit the purchase to be made
the deed and title papers for which shall be deposited
in the hands of the trustees until the party so borrow
ing the said sum or sums of money shall have paid
the same to the association the trustees having full
power and authority to adopt any other legal measure
for securing the association from loss

Article 12th

In case of the death of a member his legal represent
ative or representatives shall be entitled to receive from
out of the funds of the association the full amount of
his interest in the same subject to a deduction of
all fines and dues and the sum of two and an half
per centum on the net amount which he would be
entitled to receive

Article 13th

Any member who shall think proper to withdraw from this association having given one months notice of his intention so to do Shall be entitled to receive the amount of initiation and contribution money paid by him subject to a deduction of five percentum on the amount so paid and also to a deduction of all fines if any be due Provided nevertheless that in case the association should meet with losses or if the value of the shares should otherwise be reduced below the net amount of Initiation and dues actually paid the member or members making such demand shall in no case be allowed receive more than the net value of the share or shares held by him or them subject to such deduction as before specified

Article 14th

No member shall hold more than five shares in his own name or in that of any other persons and if any member shall be guilty of violating this article he shall forfeit to the association the share or shares of stock he may hold therein

Article 15

Every member holding one share of stock shall be entitled to one vote having two shares two votes and five shares three votes for the election of officers and on no other occasion

Article 16th

The stated meetings of this association shall be on the second monday in each and every month at such times and places as may be fixed upon by the byelaws

Article 17

No Member shall be entitled to the transfer of a loan or loans from this association for the purpose of erecting a dwelling or purchasing one at a greater

distance

distance than five miles from the market house in the Borough of Frankford nor shall any member be entitled to a loan for the purpose of building or purchasing a dwelling house unless the same be located in the County of Philadelphia

Article 18th

This association shall continue until every member shall have an opportunity of building or purchasing a dwelling house for each share of stock he may hold in the same after which the Balance in the Treasury if any shall be equally divided among the members agreeably to their respective share

Article 19th

The trustees shall at their stated meetings in January and July in each and every year appoint three of their own body a standing committee for the purpose of examining titles securing property purchased by the members and shall regulate the payment of the loans to the purchaser in such manner as they may think advisable for the interest and security of the association

Article 20th

Any member neglecting to pay his monthly contributions and fines for the term of twelve months shall forfeit to the association the amount of his interest in the same and be expelled from the society nor shall any member be entitled to claim a share from the funds thereof who may be in arrears of contributions or fines

Article 21st

No alteration or amendment shall be made to this constitution nor to the Bye laws of the association unless the same shall be proposed in writing at a stated meeting of the association to be acted upon at the next stated meeting thereafter and shall require the concurrence of two-thirds of the members present.

Pennsylvania, the first state to have a savings and loan association, continued for many years to lead the field. Seymour Dexter says:

During the last years of that decade [1840's], the organization of these associations in Philadelphia was very rapid. Until 1849 or 1850 none were incorporated. They were simply voluntary associations, holding their property through the medium of trustees. Yet so rapid had been their growth in that city that fifty or more were organized between 1831 and 1849.
... Hence it can be said with great fitness that Philadelphia has been the "breeding-place" of these associations in America.[9]

The next state to employ the savings and loan idea was New York. In 1836 a group from Brooklyn visited the Oxford Provident Association to study its operations. They apparently were pleased by what they saw, for they returned to New York to organize the Brooklyn Building and Mutual Fund Association that same year.[10] At various times the Brooklyn Building and Mutual Fund Association has been referred to as the first savings and loan association in the United States. At the present time, however, students of savings and loan history agree that the Oxford Provident Association was the earlier one. The movement spread from the New York City area to Buffalo in the 1850's.

In 1843 South Carolina organized its first savings and loan association, and in 1849, Maryland, New Jersey, and Connecticut. These three states were followed by Illinois in 1851 (early associations there were in the Chicago area), Massachusetts in 1852, Maine in 1854, and Virginia in 1859.

Map I presents the date of the first savings and loan association in each state. Once the movement was started, it continued to grow. By 1890 the subject of savings and loans was receiving attention from many quarters. In 1888 Professor Sanborn, Secretary of the American Social Science Association, made a report at the association's annual meeting, in which he said: "At the rate the building associations are now gaining, the time may come when their accumulated savings at any one time may exceed those of our savings-banks."[11] He estimated the number of associations at that time at 4,000. In 1889 Mr. Sanborn obtained additional information, upon which he based his estimate that the number was approximately 4,500, divided geographically as shown in Table 1.

[9] Seymour Dexter, *A Treatise on Co-Operative Savings and Loan Associations* (New York: Appleton and Company, 1889), pp. 43–44.
[10] Bodfish, *op. cit.*, p. 79.
[11] Dexter, *op. cit.*, p. i. Professor Sanborn's prophecy was fulfilled in 1953 when assets of savings and loan associations in the United States exceeded those of savings banks.

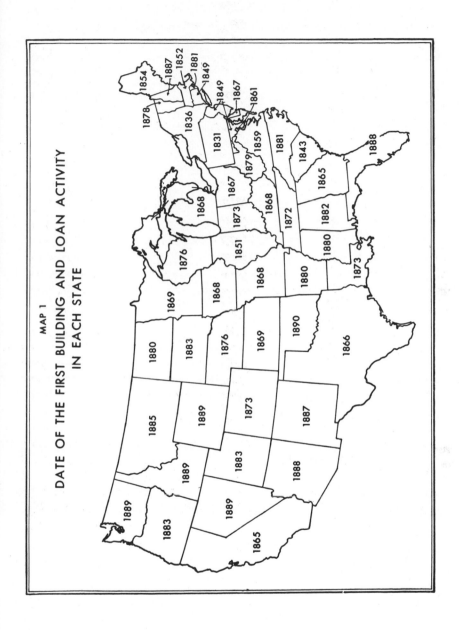

MAP 1

DATE OF THE FIRST BUILDING AND LOAN ACTIVITY IN EACH STATE

TABLE 1

SAVINGS AND LOAN ASSOCIATIONS IN THE UNITED STATES, 1889

Location	Associations
All New England	120
New York	350
New Jersey	200
Pennsylvania	950
Delaware and Maryland	225
Ohio	750
Indiana	200
Illinois	500
Wisconsin	45
Michigan	60
Minnesota	150
Iowa and Nebraska	150
Missouri	100
Kansas	130
Kentucky	100
Tennessee and the Southwest	300
Southern Atlantic States	100
California and the Northwest	150
Total	4,580

Source: *Financial Review and American Building Association News*, 13:10, January 1894.

In 1893 Carroll D. Wright, United States Commissioner of Labor, made the first government sponsored nationwide survey of the savings and loan industry. His estimates of the size of the industry are presented in Table 2.

Before leaving the topic of the growth of the savings and loan industry throughout the United States, it is necessary to pay some attention to the development of the so-called "nationals," which emerged in the later years of the last century and were to have such far-reaching effects, both good and bad, upon the industry.[12] The first of these associations appears to have been the National Building, Loan and Protective Union, which began in Minnesota around 1887.[13]

[The honor of having been the first association to enter the national] field has generally been credited to the "National of Minneapolis," but the same is contested by two other associations, one in Washington, D.C., called the "National Life Maturity Association" and another in Minneapolis, which claims the distinction of being the first orthodox or pure building and loan operated on a general plan.[14]

[12] National associations had state charters, but operated branches in many states, hence the word "national."

[13] Bodfish, *op. cit.*, p. 100.

[14] Correspondence in *The National Building and Loan Herald*, 2:16, September 15, 1890.

TABLE 2

SAVINGS AND LOAN ASSOCIATIONS IN THE UNITED STATES, 1893

Location	Associations	Shareholders	Net assets
Arkansas	69	19,493	$ 5,851,205
California	139	31,677	13,090,802
Colorado	60	16,950	5,088,004
Connecticut	15	3,222	433,578
Delaware	24	5,331	2,410,862
District of Columbia	32	24,451	6,821,861
Georgia	37	10,453	3,137,603
Florida	37	10,524	3,159,418
Illinois	518	146,571	55,821,888
Indiana	350	90,157	21,390,550
Iowa	100	36,865	9,049,310
Kansas	164	46,330	13,907,211
Louisiana	21	6,569	3,391,557
Maine	36	10,064	2,020,293
Maryland	200	62,294	14,921,607
Massachusetts	115	54,484	14,574,334
Michigan	99	27,968	8,395,207
Minnesota	91	25,708	7,716,806
Mississippi	41	11,393	3,726,291
Missouri	418	74,620	35,446,429
Nebraska	47	13,278	3,985,603
New Hampshire	17	8,857	1,137,719
New Jersey	282	87,019	30,871,644
New York	447	156,660	32,820,563
Ohio	723	227,535	59,204,826
Pennsylvania	1,100	254,918	80,860,976
Rhode Island	7	2,506	791,410
Tennessee	143	40,398	12,126,410
Utah	11	3,108	932,801
Wisconsin	67	18,928	5,681,605
All other states (estimated)	450	127,125	38,160,032
Total	5,860	1,655,456	$496,928,405

Source: *Financial Review and American Building Association News*, 13:10, January 1894.

By the late 1880's the savings and loan business had developed to a high degree, and the local associations were held in esteem by investors. National associations rode in on this wave of popularity. In the first year twelve were organized in Minnesota, and by 1893 there were 240 such associations.[15]

[15] Bodfish, *op. cit.*, p. 104.

TABLE 3

GROWTH OF SAVINGS AND LOAN ACTIVITY IN THE UNITED STATES,
1893 TO 1954

Date	Number of associations (in thousands)	Assets (in billions of dollars)	Date	Number of associations (in thousands)	Assets (in billions of dollars)
1893	5.8	.50	1923	10.7	3.9
1894	5.9	.60	1924	11.8	4.8
1895	6.0	.62	1925	12.4	5.5
1896	6.0	.65	1926	12.6	6.3
1897	5.9	.67	1927	12.8	7.2
1898	5.6	.66	1928	12.6	8.0
1899	5.6	.62	1929	12.3	8.7
1900	5.5	.60	1930	11.8	8.8
1901	5.4	.60	1931	11.4	8.4
1902	5.4	.61	1932	10.9	7.7
1903	5.3	.60	1933	10.7	7.0
1904	5.3	.62	1934	10.9	6.4
1905	5.3	.65	1935	10.5	5.9
1906	5.4	.69	1936	10.2	5.6
1907	5.5	.75	1937	9.7	5.7
1908	5.6	.80	1938	8.9	5.6
1909	5.7	.86	1939	8.3	5.7
1910	5.9	.95	1940	7.1	5.7
1911	6.1	1.00	1941	6.9	6.0
1912	6.3	1.10	1942	6.5	6.1
1913	6.4	1.20	1943	6.4	6.6
1914	6.6	1.40	1944	6.3	7.5
1915	6.8	1.50	1945	6.1	8.7
1916	7.0	1.60	1946	6.1	10.2
1917	7.3	1.80	1947	6.0	11.7
1918	7.5	1.90	1948	6.0	13.0
1919	7.8	2.10	1949	6.0	14.7
1920	8.6	2.50	1950	6.0	16.8
1921	9.3	2.90	1951	6.0	19.2
1922	10.0	3.30	1952	6.0	22.6
			1953	6.0	26.6
			1954	6.0	31.7

Sources: *Saving and Home Finance Source Book, 1954* (Washington, D.C.: Home Loan Bank Board), p. 6;
U.S. Bureau of the Census, *Historical Statistics of the United States, 1789–1945,* (Washington, D.C., 1949),
p. 175; and H. Morton Bodfish, Editor-in-Chief, *History of Building and Loan in the United States* (Chicago:
United States Building and Loan League, 1931), p. 136.

The nationals rode in on the trend of general expansion which was sweeping the country in all fields. While the small local associations had enjoyed some degree of success, it was proposed that by spreading the activities across the nation, by taking money from where it was most plentiful and investing it where it was most needed, the prospects for profits would be increased. With this premise, the nationals began what first appeared to be a campaign to dominate the savings and loan field.

Those days of direct sales of stock by savings and loan salesmen are described by Bodfish:

... A crew invaded a small town and established a branch with a local board, generally composed of persons of some prominence, including a banker and an attorney whose aid was enlisted by the promise that the local business would be thrown their way. It was announced that this "national organization" had come to the town to place a large sum of loans at once. This helped allay suspicion, so that the promises of large returns did not frighten away investors as much as might be supposed. In addition, many of the citizens were potential borrowers and so subscribed to shares in the hope of securing loans.[16]

It seems to have been a fairly common practice to use the prestige of a well-known individual, sometimes unscrupulously:

... His name [President G. Percival Steward] and influence has been used to an extraordinary degree in bolstering up and advertising the association. He it was who, as President, deposited his personal check with the association as a guarantee to stockholders that all its promises should be fulfilled. This check was photographed, and these photographic copies were circulated freely throughout the country in the hands of agents. It is reported that it proved a winning card in securing new subscribers. The eloquent agent was able to convince many unsophisticated people that the Granite State was all right beyond a doubt or the President would never risk $100,000 of his own money in guaranteeing it.[17]

As might be expected, the nationals met stiff opposition from local associations, and this opposition caused a joining of ranks to the extent that The United States League of Local Building and Loan Associations was organized in 1893, largely in an effort to fight the nationals. Savings and loan association literature of the day is filled with articles opposing the nationals. The nationals had their own organ, *The National Building and Loan Herald*, which presented the nationals' side of the argument. The *Herald* was a shabby publication which would seem to reflect discredit upon those associated with the national movement. While the primary purpose of the publication was to promote the national idea, this was done too many

[16] *Ibid.*, pp. 103–104.
[17] *Financial Review and American Building and Loan Herald*, 2:12, September 15, 1890.

times by the indirect method of attacking their enemies, the commercial banks, local savings and loan associations, and insurance companies.

The national associations attempted to give the impression that their opponents were commercial banks, insurance companies, the "Wall Street crowd," while they were out to assist the "little man." However, the "little man" did not receive especially good treatment, as is indicated by the following testimony:

. . . I joined a "National" building and loan association in order to secure a loan. For the high and mighty privilege of being a member of one of these grandiloquent associations I had to pay the modest sum of $10 on twenty-five shares and monthly payments of $15. For reasons satisfactory to themselves, and of which I will not complain, the loan was so long delayed that I finally concluded I did not want it, but I did want the money I had paid in, and how to get it was the question, and the further I inquired, the more serious it became. First, I found that I could not withdraw under one year without paying the forfeiture of all I had paid in; second, that I must continue to pay in my $15 per month until the end of the year or it would "lapse;" third, that, even if I stayed in, I could get neither interest nor profits under two years; fourth, I learned that after the expiration of the twelve months they could hold back my money for sixty days longer, which they actually did. At last, after fourteen months from my first payment, we had a settlement. I had paid in in actual cash:

Membership fee	$ 10.00
Twelve payments of $15 each	180.00
Total	$190.00
The association returned to me	$147.00
Showing a clear loss to me of	43.00
Interest on $190 for average time at 6 per cent, for twelve months would be	5.70
And for $190 for full two months at 6 per cent	1.23
Total loss	$ 49.93

Leaving out the question of interest I had to pay them 22½ per cent of my money for the time it was in their possession.[18]

The local associations fought back. Seymour Dexter, who has been referred to earlier, was extremely vocal in his opposition; presumably this was because of his sincere belief in local associations and not because he had a financial interest at stake. Largely through the activity of the League, many state laws directed against the nationals were passed. In 1893 Mr. Eckels, Comptroller of the Currency, invoked Section 5243 of the banking

[18] "National Building and Loan Associations," *Financial Review and American Building News*, 15:25, March 1896.

statutes, which prohibits the use of the word "national" in the title of a financial organization not organized under the National Banking Act.[19]

In spite of mounting opposition, the nationals continued to operate and reached their peak in 1896. But just as their rise had been spectacular, so was their decline; they went under to the accompaniment of investigations by state authorities, disclosures of fraud, severe losses to investors, and, as might be expected, an "I told you so" attitude on the part of the locals:

How are the mighty fallen. The American Savings and Loan Association of Minneapolis, perhaps the most famous of the long list of "Nationals" associations, passed into the hands of a receiver.

Readers of the *News* have heard much of the doings and troubles of the American during the past six or seven years. Its irregular business methods have at last borne the fruit that must be reaped from such a sowing.[20]

There have been many reasons advanced for the failure of the national schemes. To begin with, many national associations were fraudulent, apparently organized as fleecing devices. The stock was oftentimes misrepresented and sold to uninformed investors. Furthermore, many of the leaders were not savings and loan people. While there may be little merit in conservatism for conservatism's sake, many of the so-called conservative policies followed by savings and loan people are the results of experience. Generally speaking, the nationals either did not have or did not want to be influenced by this experience. Too, the making of direct loans throughout the whole country contributed to the weakness. Real estate is so closely tied to its neighborhood that there is a good deal to be said for local administration of loans. And finally, the approach to the problem of tying loans so directly to sales of stock would tend to make the loan policy a particularly weak one.

The rise and fall of the national movement had far-reaching effects on the savings and loan industry. The first, most obvious result of the fiasco was the detrimental effect that any large scale failures might be expected to have upon an industry as a whole. It did, for a while at least, have the undesirable effect of discrediting the industry and creating mistrust toward all savings and loan associations. However, there were also favorable results. Though the League would doubtless have come into existence eventually, the national movement hastened the organization of this association, which was to do much to raise the standards of the industry. Also, the opposition of the locals to the nationals hastened state supervision of savings and loan associations; few would deny that this was beneficial. Another improvement that doubtless would have come anyway was the nationals' development of better systems of accounting, management, and control. While the nationals

[19] *Financial Review and American Building Association News*, 12:303, December 1893.
[20] *Ibid.*, p. 3.

themselves had notoriously high operating costs, the large-scale systems which they pioneered later led to savings in operating costs.

The period of the nationals was a dark time in savings and loan history. While no one would rejoice that such a period existed, it may well be that the industry emerged stronger as a result of it.

As the savings and loan movement has grown in size, it has also evolved from a temporary undertaking to one with essentially the same degree of permanence enjoyed by other businesses. This evolution is most apparent in the plans by which the associations operate. The *plan* refers to the agreement between the association and its members which governs the life of the association and the manner in which shares will be issued and earnings distributed. In the United States four general plans have been used: the terminating plan, the serial plan, the permanent plan, and the permanent stock plan.

The plan used by the Oxford Provident Association was more or less typical of the terminating plan, which has some merit within certain limits. The terminating plan would appeal to a group with a common desire to establish an orderly method for saving and to use the money saved to buy or build homes. So long as such a group exists, there may be a place for a terminating plan. All the stock should be subscribed at the same time, and all members should share on a pro rata basis in the fund accumulated. In the event that a member desires to join after the association had operated for some time, it is necessary that he pay in enough to be on the same footing as the older members.

For best operation the plan should require that all members also borrow from the association. In fact, the usual requirement has been that only members could borrow. Of course, no return could be made on the savings unless they were lent, which may, and often did, have the effect of forcing individuals to borrow regardless of their desires. While it would easily be possible to get a group all of whom would like to make loans, this would not necessarily be the same group which would be able to contribute the most in savings. Then there is the matter of selecting the individual to receive the loan. This was usually done by a lottery or by bidding; in the latter case the member offering the highest premium received the loan.

As a matter of practical administration the system has several rather serious flaws. While it does offer a systematic savings system, usually a compulsory one enforced by assessments of fines or forfeiture of stock for failure to continue making periodic payment, there is no reason to exclude the source of funds from others who might have no wish to borrow. In practice all the stock is seldom sold at the first meeting, and the requirement that a member wishing to join at a later date would be forced to pay in enough at the time of joining to cover his pro rata share of increase in the fund might very well have the effect of excluding many who had the greatest need to belong. Too, the method of placing loans, particularly by the lottery method, may be an unhappy one. Building a home is, for most people, important enough a step that the time of doing so, within a ten year span, should not be left to chance. The use of the premium method might be somewhat better, but very little. A premium may reflect an adjustment of interest cost and probably would in a relatively free market, but the members of such an association are not in a free market. There have been instances where members were forced to take loans whether they wanted them or not.[21] Conceivably, faced with the desire to build at the moment, realizing that if he secured financing elsewhere he might still be required to accept a loan at a later date, and having a financial stake in the association which would be forfeited if he failed to continue making payments, a member might pay a premium far above what he would normally pay for the use of the money.

As serious as the limitations discussed in the above paragraph are, there is another which is even greater. In the course of operating an association, the members, chiefly the administrators, obtain valuable experience. The terminating plan, by its very nature does not allow future utilization of this experience. When the association is terminated, the experience and goodwill gained may be lost. It is possible to organize a second association and thereby salvage some of the benefits derived from experience, but to have to do so is an unnecessary impediment.

In an effort to avoid the disadvantages associated with the terminating plan, the serial plan was developed. The chief difference between the two is that while the terminating plan had only one issue of stock, which matured at a set date, almost always in ten years, the serial plan provided for periodic issues of stock, which would make it easier for members to join after the association was in operation. By continuing to bring out further series of stock, the association could achieve a degree of permanence. But here as in the terminating association the stock did mature at a certain date and was to be retired at that time. This provision would tend to militate against a long life. While the terminating plan gave each share of stock a pro rata share in the assets of the association, the serial plan did this for each series. In effect it operated as a group of terminating plans with segregation of assets.

As a rule, the serial plan dropped the requirement that all members

[21] Bodfish, *op. cit.*, p. 6.

must borrow and in so doing increased the field from which funds could be obtained. It is interesting to note that this act was the first serious departure that savings and loan associations made from prior savings and loan practice. To attain the strength which savings and loan associations were later to achieve, this departure was justified, but it does recognize that there are two distinct groups with an interest in the affairs of an association and the interests of the two are not served best by the same policy. Hence, a co-operative association is not the most efficient in this field.

The serial plan was a great improvement over the older terminating plan, but it, too, had some rather serious faults. The maturing stock, even when issued in series, was payable at stated intervals, and many times the payment of such large amounts would seriously interrupt the lending activities of the association for an extended period before and after the maturity date.

Because each series was handled, in effect, as a separate business, the record keeping problems were magnified. Inasmuch as many associations were administered, particularly in their formative years, by individuals with little accounting training, the complicated records were doubtless a serious handicap. Though the serial plan associations were able to develop fairly simple and complete accounting systems, as associations grew in size, accounting continued to be one of their more difficult problems.

The next step in the evolution of the various plans of operation, the permanent plan, was a refinement and improvement upon the serial plan. The permanent plan provided for a sale of stock at any time an individual wished to purchase it. It eliminated the necessity of either waiting until date of issue or else paying in a pro rata share of increase. In so doing, it made it as easy to open an account with a savings and loan association as with a bank. While the idea of maturity persisted, the effect was to achieve a more or less gradual and steady redemption of stock rather than large periodic ones. Nor did the permanent associations require that stock be redeemed at maturity. While there was still technical maturity of shares, the effect was to give a large percentage of the shares the permanence of a savings account in a bank. It would seem to make for a smoother operation.

Also the permanent plan provided for crediting of dividends to the accounts at specific intervals, usually semiannually, and eliminated the segregation of accounts. In order to do this, it was necessary to retain some of the earnings to provide for future losses and other contingencies. This was accomplished by either a reserve for contingencies or an undivided profits account. The use of these accounts represented a fairly serious departure from prior savings and loan theory. Until the emergence of the permanent plans, all profits accrued and were eventually paid to the shareholders. The effect of using a reserve or fund was to place some of the assets beyond the reach of the shareholders so that if they did benefit from them, other than in liquidation, it would be the indirect benefit of greater stability provided by such a reserve. In order to operate efficiently, such a plan was needed; it may have been necessary to the development of a strong savings and loan industry, although it represented another departure from the practices of the early associations. The permanent plan, as described above, is essentially the one employed by today's federal associations.

The fourth and last plan to emerge was the permanent stock or guaranteed stock plan. This plan takes the savings and loan association one step closer to other corporations and one step farther from the mutual idea. In essence the plan is this: at the time of organization a certain amount of the stock which is not withdrawable is sold to investors. The investors may resell the stock to other investors if they so desire. The permanent stock, since it can not be withdrawn, is to act as a cushion or buffer against loss on the part of other investors or savers.

In addition to the nonwithdrawable feature, permanent stock also receives different treatment for dividend purposes. There is no set dividend which applies to permanent stock; it need not be, and seldom is, at the same rate which applies to ordinary stock. In the early years of an association there may be no dividend on the permanent stock. As the association prospers, the dividend may far exceed the rate paid on ordinary stock.[22] It is probably impossible to ascertain which of two reasons accounts for the use of a permanent stock plan: the desire to provide a better protected investment for the ordinary stockholders or the desire to provide a high yield from the investment of the original organizers. The latter is probably the stronger motivating force, even though the former is automatically achieved when permanent stock represents a large enough percentage of all stock.

Many states, Texas included, allow the requirement that a majority or all of the board of directors be selected from the permanent stockholders. Because the ownership of permanent stock is customarily not widely diffused, this has the effect of facilitating control by a small group. All members must and do have the right to vote for directors, but they are restricted in whom they may elect.

Of the four plans discussed, the last two have the most to offer, both to the organizers and to the future stockholders or investors. However, to select one of the last two, either the permanent plan or the permanent stock plan, is more difficult. From the administrator's point of view the permanent stock plan, which makes it easier to maintain control and thereby, particularly in times of stress, to follow sounder management policies, would

[22] In Texas, a state association may not pay a dividend on permanent stock during the first three years after organization.

seem to be the better. Also, since the administrators are usually also the holders of the permanent stock, the possibility of large dividends on the permanent stock is an incentive. Generally, borrowers are treated alike regardless of whether the permanent or permanent stock plan is used.

From the savers' point of view, the permanent plan, particularly at first glance, might seem to have more to recommend it. To begin with, all shareholders are on the same footing, and all stock shares equally in dividends. In addition, the members have greater freedom in electing directors, for all members, if they meet the provisions of the by-laws, are eligible for directorship. Actually, these advantages to stockholders may be more illusive than real. While there is an equal sharing of dividends by all stock, a large percentage of the profits may be drained off by the administrators in the form of salaries, services, fringe benefits, and the like, to the end that the stockholders in the permanent plan association may receive essentially the same remuneration that they would receive in a permanent stock plan. Another reason that this is true is explained by the attitude of the savings and loan people toward dividends. They seem to consider dividends as payment for the use of money and not as a return of profits to the investors. They gauge their dividend rate according to the market interest rate and raise it or lower it in response to changes in interest rates rather than in response to profitableness. So far as voting rights are concerned, stockholders in a permanent association, it is true, do have the right to vote for whomsoever they may choose to represent them on the board of directors, but the voting right may not mean much. Customarily, use of proxy voting by the management coupled with lethargy on the part of most investors has the effect of removing the voting advantage enjoyed by a stockholder in a permanent plan association over that enjoyed by an ordinary stockholder in a permanent stock plan association.

CHAPTER III

Development of Savings and Loan Associations in Texas, 1866–1916

The main purpose of this book has been to trace the development of the savings and loan industry in Texas as well as other changes which have either encouraged or supplemented its development. In a broad sense, there is scarcely a segment of economic activity in Texas which has not in some manner affected savings and loan development. This study, however, has necessarily been restricted to the history of the industry, state and federal legislation relating to savings and loan associations, and such other factors as bear most directly upon the subject.

The first period of savings and loan activity in Texas, from 1866 to 1916, is the longest but probably the least important of the five periods to be discussed. In order to explain the early savings and loan movement in the state, the beginning in 1866, and the subsequent cessation until after 1874, it is necessary to trace the political history of the state.

At the close of the Civil War, Texas was placed under military rule. President Andrew Johnson, however, issued an amnesty proclamation proposing to allow ,Texas and the other confederate states to re-enter the Union as rapidly as possible. On June 6, 1866, an election was held to adopt or reject a new Texas Constitution and to elect state, district, and county officers and representatives. James W. Throckmorton defeated Elisha M. Pease in a four-to-one victory to become the first elected governor after the war. Mr. Throckmorton, it is interesting to note, was one of seven who voted against secession among the 174 delegates to the secession convention in 1861. Even though Mr. Throckmorton opposed secession, once the state had seceded, he supported the southern cause, became an officer in the Army of the Confederacy, and returned a war hero.

Governor Throckmorton was inaugurated in August, 1866; he and the Eleventh Legislature represented essentially the same group that had controlled the state politically before the war. It was during this brief administration that the first corporate savings and loan association in Texas was chartered. It first appeared that the transition to full statehood was to be an easy one, but within a few months, obstacles to the transition began to appear. In February of 1867, Congress declared:

. . . 'the present pretended' state governments of these states to be 'null and void' as, it was declared, 'they are under the control of unrepentant leaders of the

Rebellion;' and, further, that it was necessary that peace and good order should be enforced by the military, in the so-called States until loyal and Republican State governments should be legally formed.[1]

In July the erstwhile antisecessionist Governor ,Throckmorton was removed from office after being declared "an impedement to the reconstruction of Texas under the law."[2] Elisha Pease was appointed in his place. Pease, a union sympathizer, had remained in Austin during the war and apparently took no part in the hostilities. He had previously opposed Governor Throckmorton in the 1866 election and was defeated by a four-to-one margin. Thus began the reconstruction period in Texas. Pease was shortly succeeded by Edmund J. Davis, who held the office of governor until 1874.

At the time of Governor Throckmorton's administration there was no general savings and loan law; it required a special act of the legislature to charter such an organization. On November 6, 1866, the Texas Legislature passed its first such bill, one introduced by Mr. Brady, which provided:

Section 1. Be it enacted by the Legislature of the State of Texas, that James B. Cato, E. A. Bolmes, E. H. Gaylord, E. A. Herndon, W. D. Cleveland, W. R. Webb, R. Green, Jr., S. W. Sydnor, E. L. Hopkins and C. S. Marston, and their associates and successors, are hereby created and established a body corporate and politic, under the name and style of the "Young Men's Mutual Real Estate and Building Association," with capacity in said corporate name to make contracts; to hold, buy, and sell property, both real and personal; to contract and execute leases; to take grants and gifts; to execute deeds, mortgages and deeds of trust; to have succession, and a common seal; to make by-laws for the government and regulation of its affairs; to sue and be sued; to plead and be impleaded; to declare dividends, and make divisions of property; to do and perform all such things as may be necessary and proper for or incident to the fulfillment of its obligations and maintenance of its rights under this Act, and consistant with Constitution and laws of the State; provided, that the operations of said association, as to the purchase or holding of real property, shall be restricted exclusively to and within the county of Harris.

Section 2. The officers and managers of this association shall consist of seven directors and one treasurer, to be elected by the shareholders. There shall be one President and one Vice President, to be chosen from and by the board of directors; and also one Secretary, to be selected by the directors from the shareholders. Such officers shall receive such compensation as the by-laws may provide, their term of office shall be for one year, subject to removal in such manner as the by-laws may prescribe.

Section 3. The capital stock shall be sixty thousand ($60,000) dollars, with the power and privilege of increasing the same to three hundred, thousand ($300,000) dollars.

Section 4. This association shall not own and possess, at any one time, real property in the State of Texas, exceeding in value one million dollars.

[1] John Henry Brown, *History of Texas, From 1865 to 1892* (St. Louis: L. E. Daniell, 1893), p. 446.
[2] *Ibid.*, p. 447.

Section 5. The capital stock of sixty thousands dollars shall be divided into one hundred shares of six hundred dollars per share, payable in monthly installments of ten ($10) dollars per month.

Section 6. Any shareholder who fails, neglects, or refuses to pay or cause to be paid his regular monthly installment, his stock shall be forfeited to the association; provided, however, that by and with the consent of the board of directors, for good cause shown, such delinquent may be allowed fifteen days to redeem stock thus forfeited.

Section 7. No person shall own more than one share of stock in this association and the number of shares shall be one hundred; and in case any share of stock shall become forfeited in accordance with the foregoing provisions, the board of directors shall dispose of the same to the highest bidder, in such manner as the by-laws may direct.

Section 8. Whenever one hundred shares shall have been subscribed, and two months' installments paid in, this association shall be deemed organized and competent to transact business under this charter, and be entitled to all grants and privileges hereunder.

Section 9. Service of any and all legal proceedings, in any suit or proceedings against said company, shall be sufficient if made upon the President or Secretary of the board of directors.

Section 10. This Act or Charter shall remain in full force and effect from and after the date of its passage, for and during the period of twenty years.[3]

There may have been unincorporated savings and loan associations in Texas before 1866, but no record of prior associations could be found.[4]

By today's standards the Young Men's Mutual Real Estate and Building Association of Houston would hardly be considered a savings and loan association; it was more in the nature of a real estate company. This seems, however, to have been fairly typical of the early associations. In describing the status of the savings and loan industry in several states, an article in the *Financial Review* says:

This State [Texas] has on its statute books no laws relating especially to the building and loan business. As stated last year, the trend there is more to real estate investment companies, on a co-operative basis, which have achieved eminent success. The Supreme Court of the State some years ago decided adversely to the legality of deducting premiums, and the associations conduct their business by charging a straight interest of 10 per cent. The associations pay a corporation tax of $10, and all stock must be assessed the same as other stocks are assessed, presumably at actual value.[5]

There was little savings and loan activity during the early reconstruction period. In 1870 T. McMahon, a Galveston banker, was able to obtain a

[3] *General Laws of the State of Texas, Eleventh Legislature, 1866* (Austin: Jo. Walker, at State Gazette Office, 1866), pp. 266–267.

[4] A thorough study of census reports and other historical data as well as writings of others treating the history of savings and loan activity in Texas failed to disclose any savings and loans associations in the state prior to 1866.

[5] *Financial Review*, Vol. 14, Nov. 1895, p. 21.

charter for the Island City Real Estate and Homestead Association, which had a capital of $75,000.[6] Bodfish lists nine other associations formed about this time but notes that "the names of these companies indicate that many of them had real estate investment aspects and were not pure building and loan concerns."[7]

As said before, the reconstruction officially ended in Texas in 1874, and there was an immediate increase in the number of new associations formed. Table 4 lists the associations organized between December 1874 and April 1876.

Ray A. Benson, the current Savings and Loan Supervisor in Texas in a speech delivered to the Texas Savings and Loan League states:

> Beginning in the early eighties, building and loan associations operated as partnerships or corporations under general laws of the state until 1913.[8]

Mr. Benson updated the beginning of the savings and loan movement in ,Texas to the 1880's because it was not until then that groups began to take on characteristics of true savings and loan associations. In 1880 the Dallas Homestead and Loan Association was organized; this association operated for over fifty years and was finally liquidated and dissolved on July 19, 1938. Because savings and loan associations were not required to report to any agency, there are no available statistics for the early years.

In 1888 Professor Robert T. Hill of Austin estimated the number of associations operating in Texas at fifty.[9] But in view of subsequent findings his estimate seems high.

In 1893 the first comprehensive study of savings and loan associations in the United States, referred to in an earlier chapter, was made by Carroll D. Wright, United States Commissioner of Labor. At that time, there were thirty-nine local associations and two national ones. Of the thirty-nine local associations, twenty-one were less than five years old, sixteen were between five and ten years old, and the remaining two were over ten but under fifteen years old.[10] Table 5 presents a consolidated balance sheet for the thirty-nine local associations operating in Texas, and Table 6 classifies them on the basis of real estate loans. Most of these association were small; only three had more than 300 members, and only four had as many as 100 borrowers.[11]

---

[6] H. Morton Bodfish (ed.), *History of Building and Loan in the United States* (Chicago: United States Building and Loan League, 1931), p. 576.

[7] *Ibid.*

[8] Address delivered by Ray A. Benson to the Texas Savings and Loan League, Austin, 1952.

[9] *Journal of Social Sciences*, 24:156, 1888.

[10] *Ninth Annual Report of the Commissioner of Labor*, 1893 (Washington, D.C.: Government Printing Office, 1894), p. 338.

[11] *Ibid.*, pp. 292–295.

TABLE 4

TEXAS SAVINGS AND LOAN ASSOCIATIONS ORGANIZED, 1874 TO 1876

County	Name of corporation	Date of organization
Galveston	Galveston Daymen's Benevolent Association	12- 9-74
Comanche	Real Estate Building and Loan Company	12-28-74
Galveston	First German Ladies' Benevolent Association	12-30-74
Navarro	Corsicana Real Estate and Savings Association	2- 6-75
Freestone	Texas Homestead and Building Association	2-18-75
Fayette	Fayette County Real Estate and Building Association	2-19-75
Limestone	Hebrew Benevolent Society of Mexia	3- 1-75
Travis	Laboring Men's Mutual Aid of North Texas	3- 6-75
Harris	Houston Land and Trust Company	4-24-75
Harrison	Mechanics' Co-operative Association of Marshall	4- 6-75
Travis	Texas Real Estate and Colonization Company	4-15-75
Washington	Brenham Immigration Benevolent Club	6-26-75
Harris	Lone Star State Immigrant Labor Bureau and Real Estate, Loan, Trust and Deposit Company	7-19-75
Ellis	Waxahachie Real Estate and Savings Association	1-19-76
Caldwell	Luling Real Estate, Building and Loan Association	2- 9-76
Harris	Young Men's Mutual Real Estate and Building Association	2-22-76
Leon	Jewett Building Association	3- 6-76
Dallas	Dallas Savings and Loan Association	3-16-76

Source: Records of the Secretary of State of Texas.

Six of the associations organized prior to 1913, when savings and loan associations were placed under the supervision of the Commissioner of Insurance and Banking, are still in business today. These are:[12] Taylor Building & Loan Association, Taylor, chartered May 15, 1885; Sulphur Springs Loan & Building Association, Sulphur Springs, chartered August 13, 1890; San Saba Building & Loan Association, San Saba, chartered September 27, 1890; Hesperian Building & Loan Association, Gainesville, chartered November 14, 1890; Mutual Building & Loan Association, Weatherford, chartered March 27, 1891; and Hearne Building & Loan Association, Hearne, chartered March 22, 1909.[13]

In 1897 the first organization of a Texas League was accomplished, with W. G. Bell of Austin serving as president. Mr. Bell was a director of a savings and loan association, as the following letter indicates:

[12] Benson, *op. cit.*
[13] A detailed listing of the savings and loan associations operating in Texas in 1893 is presented in Appendix.

TABLE 5

ASSETS AND LIABILITIES OF THIRTY-NINE LOCAL TEXAS
SAVINGS AND LOAN ASSOCIATIONS, 1893

Assets

Real estate loans	$1,642,335
Share loans	51,899
Other secured loans	50,162
Cash on hand	78,910
Other assets	121,567
Total assets	$1,944,873*

Liabilities

Borrowed money	$ 29,413
Dues paid on instalment shares	1,483,098
Profits	379,183
Paid-up stock	17,469
Other liabilities	35,710
Total liabilities	$1,944,873

Source: Ninth Annual Report of the Commissioner of Labor, 1893 (Washington, D.C.: Government Printing Office, 1894), pp. 316–17.
* At this time Texas also had two national associations with total assets of $239,526.

TABLE 6

THIRTY-NINE LOCAL TEXAS SAVINGS AND LOAN ASSOCIATIONS, 1893,
CLASSIFIED ACCORDING TO REAL ESTATE LOANS

Total loans	Associations
Under $25,000	17
More than $25,000, under $50,000	9
Over $50,000, under $75,000	5
Over $75,000, under $100,000	6
Over $100,000, under $125,000	1
Over $125,000, under $150,000	0
Over $150,000, under $175,000	1
Total	39

Source: Ninth Annual Report of the Commissioner of Labor, 1893 (Washington, D.C.: Government Printing Office, 1894), pp. 300–301.

Editor News:

Dear Sir:—Our Local Building and Loan Association of this city, of which I am a director, is anxious to place a few hundred shares of prepaid stock at $50 per share, 8 per cent interest, payable semi-annually, stock to pay out in about 125 months.

We can furnish a full statement of our last years' business to any one who desires such. We realize, money brings lower rates of interest in the States, and to this end believe our investment to be A 1, and worthy of investigation.

Will you oblige a subscriber of the News by giving me the names of eight or ten capitalists; also of reliable stock brokers who would place our stock in sums of $5,000, $10,000, and upwards.

We have a splendid field to work on. Ours is the *only home* association in the city. We have 26,000 inhabitants. The demand for money to build is very heavy. Please give this matter your early attention, and oblige,

Yours truly,
Wm. G. Bell.[14]

The high interest rates referred to by Mr. Bell were high indeed.

It was not uncommon for a borrower to pay a premium of 50 per cent for a loan, in other words, receive 50¢ for each dollar borrowed. In addition to paying two for one for the cash received, notes drew interest at the rate of at least 6 per cent per annum. . . .[15]

The associations operating in 1880's, and 1890's were mostly local organizations operating under the terminating plan. Few operated under the serial plan, fewer still under the permanent plan. Because of the predominance of the terminating plan, many of the associations went out of business. In the 1893 report of the Commissioner of Labor, referred to earlier, Texas had a total of thirty-nine local associations; of these, twenty used the terminating plan, seventeen used the serial plan, and two used the permanent plan.[16]

The by-laws usually permitted the sale of both paid-up shares and instalment shares. When shares were paid for in instalments, the payments were set at fifty cents or a dollar a share per month. The associations customarily charged monthly dues of five or ten cents a share, and many charged an admission or membership fee. Associations also charged a late penalty or fine, usually 1 percent, on late monthly payments. The monthly instalments were treated as shares and, as such, were available for loans; but the fines, fees, and dues were treated as income and were used to defray costs of operation. In case a borrower failed to continue making his payments, his shares were forfeited. After charging the account for all dues, late fines, and other charges, what remained was returned to the investor. Many associations also charged a high withdrawal fee if shares were withdrawn before being fully paid up.

It was hoped that the effect of the numerous fees, fines, and dues would be to insure a steady flow of funds into an association. Certainly, a saver

[14] Correspondence, *Financial Review and American Building Association News*, 13:269, November, 1894.

[15] Benson, *op. cit.*

[16] *Ninth Annual Report of the Commissioner of Labor, 1893* (Washington, D.C.: Government Printing Office, 1894), p. 280.

suffered severe penalties if he failed to continue his payments. But apparently the plan had the effect of deterring many savers who feared the risk of being committed to a fixed monthly payment with such severe penalties if payments were discontinued.

As already mentioned, associations provided for two methods of selling stock; however, the method employed in lending tended to create three types of shareholders: the investor who bought paid-up shares, the small saver who chose a savings and loan association because it would accept small amounts, and the borrower who was required to subscribe to stock. In this period the sinking-fund method of lending was quite commonly employed. The sinking-fund method, which persisted until the 1930's, worked in the following manner: A borrower was required to subscribe to stock in the amount of his loan. As periodic payments were made, rather than reducing the amount of the loan they were applied to the purchase of shares. The association paid its customary dividend upon these shares but usually at a rate considerably lower than the interest charged. The net effect was to raise the actual interest cost above what it would have been if a principal retirement plan had been used.

Early Texas associations used both the premium and drawing methods of allocating loans. Of the two, the more commonly used method was to set aside certain days of each month on which accumulated funds would be offered to members who paid the highest premium. The bidding was open, and members bid against one another to secure the funds. Some associations accepted sealed bids, to be opened by the directors as funds accumulated. By 1893 twenty-eight of the thirty-nine local associations operating in Texas held no public auction and charged no premium of any sort but did use the sinking-fund method.[17] Of the remaining eleven, ten awarded the loans to the highest bidders, and one association held drawings to determine who would receive loans.[18]

During the 1890's several court actions were brought against savings and loan associations: "cause of the suit—usury; verdicts were rendered in favor of the plaintiff."[19] In spite of the poor treatment received by borrowers, savings and loan associations were not generally held in disrepute. Those were days of high interest rates in Texas, regardless of the source of a loan. Intead of considering their treatment of borrowers as a condemnation of the industry, it can more properly be taken as a gauge of the progress that the savings and loan industry has made since that time.

[17] *Ibid.*, p. 388.
[18] For a detailed listing of the associations operating in Texas in 1893, see Appendix.
[19] Benson, *op. cit.*

By the turn of the century, the more progressive savings and loan associations were taking notice of the abuses that existed within their industry. Many of them proposed some method of policing the industry. The results of this attitude culminated in the 1913 law providing for the supervision of savings and loan associations. Mr. J. L. Penry is generally credited with instigating the passage of this act, providing for regulation and supervision of savings and loan assocations. Though deficient on many points, the act did much to raise the standards of savings and loan operations and to improve the public relations of the industry.

Within this period a second attempt was made to obtain the benefits to be derived from a league. The first league, already mentioned, existed for only a short time. In 1915 a second league was organized; but it, too, was unsuccessful. It was not until the 1920's that a permanent league was organized.

CHAPTER IV

Texas Legislation Affecting Savings and Loan Associations, 1913–1953

Prior to 1913 each savings and loan association in Texas was chartered by a special act of the Legislature. In 1913 the Thirty-third Legislature at its first called session, July 21 to August 19, passed House Bill No. 17:

An Act to provide for the incorporation and regulation of certain corporations generally known as building and loan associations; and for the government and control of the same; placing the same under the control and supervision of the Commissioner of Insurance and Banking; and providing for the admission into this State of Foreign building and loan associations; and providing penalties for the violation of this act, . . .[1]

House Bill No. 17 was the first general law pertaining to savings and loan associations passed in Texas; for this reason, and because it was the law which, with slight changes, governed savings and loan activity over the next sixteen years, it deserves detailed consideration.

The act provided that:

Section 1. Any number of persons, not less than five, who are residents of this State, desiring to organize a building and loan association for the purpose of building and improving homesteads, removing incumbrances therefrom, and loaning money to the members thereof, may, by complying with the provisions of this Act, and entering into articles of association, become a corporate body. Said articles of association shall be signed by persons associating and acknowledged before some person authorized by the laws of this State to take acknowledgments to deeds, and shall set forth:

First, the name assumed by the association, which shall not be the same assumed by any other association incorporated under this Act, nor so similar as to be liable to mislead.

Second, the purpose for which the association is formed.

Third, the amount of its authorized capital stock; and the number of shares into which it is divided; the par value of each share; and the number of shares subscribed for, which shall not be less than fifty in number.

Fourth, the names of the incorporators; their respective residences and the number of shares subscribed by each.

Fifth, the term of its corporate existence, which shall not exceed fifty years.

Sixth, the name of the town, city or village in which such association is to be located.[2]

[1] *General and Special Laws of the State of Texas, Thirty-third Legislature, First Called Session 1913* (Austin, 1913), p. 72.
[2] *Ibid.*

Thus, savings and loan associations organized under the 1913 act were given permission to engage in many activities other than the one now accepted as their prime fuction: making loans on improved urban real estate. Savings and loan associations were allowed to carry on essentially the same development and sales projects that land companies might have engaged in. It will be recalled that the early special-chartered savings and loan associations of Texas resembled, in this respect, land companies more than they did savings and loan associations.

In order to organize an association under the 1913 act, it was necessary to submit a proposed title; the words "building and loan" did not have to appear therein. This was probably a rather serious oversight. One of the advantages claimed for state regulation or supervision is that the State, by its regulation, enforces certain standards that contribute to the protection of those who invest in regulated institutions. This advantage may be largely lost if the title of the institution is not distinctive enough to differentiate it from others.

While the 1913 act did require that in its application for a charter, an association must state the amount of its capital stock and the par value, associations were allowed to select a par value of not less than twenty-five dollars nor more than two hundred dollars.[3] Associations were permitted to issue their stock in series or at any time not in conflict with the by-laws. In addition, it was permissible to issue new shares to replace matured shares, provided the total issue did not exceed the amount in Section 1, paragraph 3. In the event that an association desired to increase the total amount of its capital stock, the following provision permitted it to do so:

. . . any building and loan association heretofore or hereafter incorporated under the laws of this State, may, by a resolution adopted by a two-thirds vote of shares represented and voted at an annual meeting, or at any meeting called for that purpose, increase its authorized capital stock and shares, . . . but no such increase of authorized capital stock nor amendments shall have effect until a copy of such resolution, certified by the president and secretary of such association, shall be filed, approved and recorded in the same manner as is provided in section two of this Act filed with the Secretary of State and a copy furnished to the Commissioner of Insurance and Banking for the filing and recording of original articles of association and the filing and approval of by-laws.[4]

House Bill No. 17 provided that the capital stock was to be divided into shares "payable in periodic installments, called dues, not exceeding two dollars per month on each share."[5] At this time, stock was customarily sold on the instalment plan, even though it was permissible to make advance

[3] *Ibid.*, p. 73.
[4] *Ibid.*, pp. 73–74.
[5] *Ibid.*, p. 73.

payments. While some stock is still sold on the instalment plan, this method is no longer common.[6]

The duration of the charter of associations organized under the 1913 act was fifty years, but the following provision made it possible to extend the life of the association:

Any loan or building association incorporated under this Act, or any prior act, may extend the duration of time for which said association was organized by a vote of two-thirds of the capital stock of such association, or at any special meeting called for that purpose; thereupon the board of directors shall transmit a copy of the proceedings of such annual meeting or of such special meeting, duly attested, to the Secretary of State, who shall make a duly authenticated copy thereof, as provided in said section three of this Act, certifying to the extension of time of such corporation, and the same shall be filed with the Commissioner of Insurance and Banking and recorded as provided in said section three of this Act, and any building and loan association incorporated under any prior act presumably a special act of incorporation, and extending the time for which it was incorporated, in the manner herein provided, shall be deemed as incorporated under and be invested with all the power given in this Act, the same as though such Corporation had been originally incorporated under it.[7]

The act of 1913 did not specifically require that all savings and loan associations, except foreign savings and loan associations, come under this particular act. The act was designed to apply to savings and loan associations yet to be organized and to those that had been in existence for a short time, not to those which had operated for some time. However, inasmuch as all of the savings and loan associations then existing had terminating charters, the section quoted above had the effect of eventually bringing all associations under the act.

Section 2 of House Bill No. 17 required that:

When executed as aforesaid, said articles of association shall be approved by, and filed with the Secretary of State, and a copy thereof, duly authenticated under the hand and seal of State, shall be delivered to the Commissioner of Insurance and Banking, who shall file the same in his office, and a like copy thereof shall be recorded in the office of the clerk of the county court of the county in which the principal office of such association is located; whereupon the persons named in the articles of association, their associates and successors, shall become a corporate body for the period for which they were organized, and shall exercise such powers as are herein granted, and such other powers as are necessary to enable such association to carry out the purpose of its organization, not inconsistent with the provisions of this Act; provided, that before such association shall proceed to business it shall adopt by-laws for the regulation and management of its business. Said by-laws shall not become operative until a copy thereof, duly certified by the

[6] Technically, this occurs with a savings account which is added to periodically; however, few fixed commitment instalment contracts are used currently.

[7] *Op. cit.*, pp. 75–76.

president and secretary of the association shall have been approved by and filed with the Commissioner of Insurance and Banking, and when so approved and filed the said Commissioner of Insurance and Banking shall issue his certificate of such approval and filing and thereupon said association may proceed to business. The provisions of this Act shall not apply to loan corporations heretofore incorporated under the laws of Texas loaning money on real estate, or improvements thereon, in cities of this State of more than thirty thousand inhabitants and not requiring the borrowers to be members thereof, or holders of shares in such corporations, and which have been doing business for as long as ten years prior to the passage of this Act.[8]

Section 2 gave the Secretary of State the power to approve or reject applications for organizations. Yet, the Commissioner of Insurance and Banking was not given the power to reject an application. It is true that an association could not begin operations until a copy of the proposed by-laws had been approved by the Commissioner of Insurance and Banking, but this was at best, a weak instrument of control. Seemingly, the only control which the Commissioner had over the organization of an association was the rather dubious authority to require that the by-laws be properly phrased. In effect, the regulatory agency was destined to sit idly by and wait until trouble developed before it could do anything about it. It might almost be stated as a maxim that regulatory bodies can perform as great a service by preventing the organization of certain associations as they can by policing those already organized. Section 2 of House Bill No. 17 thus seriously impaired the effectiveness of regulation and supervision of Texas savings and loan associations.

The responsibility for supervising savings and loan associations was vested in the Commissioner of Insurance and Banking by the following provisions:

> The Commissioner of Insurance and Banking shall have supervision of all building and loan associations doing business in this State, and shall be charged with the execution of the laws of this State relating to such associations; . . .[9]

Associations operating under the 1913 act were required to file annual statements with the Commissioner. No mention was made in the law of the nature of these financial reports: were they to be public information or were they to be confidential? The issue was not settled until 1929.

Provision was made for periodic examination of the savings and loan associations through the following provision:

> Section 16. Once in each year, or oftener, if in the opinion of the Commissioner of Insurance and Banking it shall be necessary the Commissioner of Insurance and Banking shall make or cause to be made, an examination into the affairs of all building and loan associations doing business in this State. Such examinations

[8] *Ibid.*, p. 77.
[9] *Ibid.*, p. 76.

shall be full and complete, and in making the same the examiner shall have full access to, and may compel the production of all books, papers and moneys, etc., of the association under examination, and may administer oaths to and examine the officers of such association or any other person connected therewith, as to its business and affairs.

The Commissioner of Insurance and Banking may appoint such special examiners as may be necessary to carry out the provisions of this Act. Such examiner shall be paid at the rate of eight dollars per day; they shall also receive necessary traveling expenses connected with the duties of their office, which shall be paid by the State Treasurer on the warrant of the Commissioner of Insurance and Banking and the approval of the Governor.[10]

In the event that an examination disclosed a state of insolvency, or that an association was conducting its affairs in an unsafe or unlawful manner, the Commissioner of Insurance and Banking was directed to appraise the board of directors of the fact and to give them twenty days to correct the situation. Then, if the directors failed to do what was necessary to right the affairs of the association, the Commissioner of Insurance and Banking was empowered to:

... order one of the examiners, appointed to examine such association, or a special examiner appointed for the purpose, to take possession of all books, records and assets of every description of such association and hold and retain possession of the same pending the further proceedings hereinafter specified. Should the board of directors, secretary or person in charge of such association refuse to permit the said examiner to take possession aforesaid, said Commissioner shall communicate such fact to the Attorney General, whereupon the Attorney General shall at once institute such proceedings as may be necessary to place such examiner in immediate possession of the property of such association. Upon taking possession of the effects of the association as aforesaid, said examiner shall prepare a full and true statement of the affairs and conditions of such association, including an itemized statement of its assets and liabilities, and shall receive and collect all debts, dues and claims belonging to it, and may pay the immediate and reasonable expense of his trust. Said examiner shall be required to execute to the Commissioner of Insurance and Banking a good and sufficient bond, conditioned for the faithful discharge of his duties as custodian of such association, which said bond shall be approved by said Commissioner.[11]

In addition to the above points contained in the 1913 act, there were also provisions for certain fairly routine matters affecting the administration of savings and loan associations: requirements for the directors, frequency of meetings, rights and duties of shareholders and borrowers, the legal status of the association, and other points which were to control the operation and administration of savings and loan associations. The act also required that foreign savings and loan associations submit to essentially the same degree of regulation and supervision as the domestically chartered associations.

[10] *Ibid.*, pp. 76–77.
[11] *Ibid.*, p. 77.

The next piece of legislation which affected savings and loan associations was passed by the second called session of the Thirty-eighth Legislature, which convened on April 16, 1923, and adjourned the following May 15. In this session, Senate Bill No. 82 was passed to provide for:

> . . . a Department of Banking for the State of Texas separate from the Department of Insurance of this State, to provide for the appointment, term of office, official name, compensation and to prescribe the qualifications, powers and duties of the head of such Department.[12]

The passage of this act was the culmination of a long struggle, both in and out of the Texas Legislature. Mr. Ed Hall, the Commissioner of Insurance and Banking, writing his letter of transmittal for the 1922 annual report to Governor Pat M. Neff stated:

> It has been recommended by practically every Commissioner of this Department that the Department of Insurance and Banking be separated. The Legislature, at one time, passed a bill to separate the departments, but the then Governor, the Honorable W. P. Hobby, for reasons best known to himself, vetoed such bill. I sincerely and earnestly recommend that this Department be separated into a Department of Banking and a Department of Insurance. The two are not related. A man competent to fill one position is not necessarily competent to fill the other. Even though he be a man competent to fill both positions, the enormous amount of work and the size to which both departments have grown since the enactment of their respective laws, places a burden upon one man which he cannot successfully carry for any considerable period. The State bankers and the insurance companies are, practically unanimous in desiring this separation. It should be effected at the earliest possible moment.[13]

Apparently the reasons best known to Governor Hobby were also known to Governor Neff, for he too vetoed the first such bill passed by the Thirty-eighth Legislature.[14] However, the second, Senate Bill 82, did pass.

Senate Bill No. 82 was specific in naming the powers and duties of the newly created office of Commissioner of Banking, in that it provided:

> The Department of Banking herein created and the Banking Commissioner of Texas herein provided for as the head thereof shall have and exercise all of the powers, privileges and duties now under the law devolving upon the Commissioner of Insurance and Banking with reference to the business of banking in this State, and in so far as supervision of the State Banking System of Texas is concerned, but said Commissioner shall have nothing to do with the administration of the Insurance laws of this State; wherever in the laws of Texas now written in connection with the control and supervision of the State banks and State Banking

[12] *General Laws of the State of Texas, 38th Legislature, 1st, 2nd, and 3rd Called Sessions, 1923* (Austin, 1923), p. 107.

[13] *Forty-seventh Annual Report of the Commissioner of Insurance, Pertaining to Banking, 1922* (Austin, 1922), p. 4.

[14] Frank A. Ross, *Texas Banking Legislation, 1833–1953* (Ph.D. dissertation, The University of Texas, Austin, 1954), p. 226.

System of Texas is concerned, the term, "Commissioner of Insurance, and Banking" is used, said term shall be construed to mean the "Banking Commissioner of Texas" as created by this act.[15]

Nowhere in the above act is there any mention of savings and loan associations. Presumably, if an institution is not a bank it is an insurance company. By failing to mention savings and loan associations, Senate Bill No. 82 left them under the supervision of what was to become the Insurance Commission.

The second called session of the Forty-first Legislature, which convened on June 3, 1929, and adjourned on July 2, passed Senate Bill No. 111, a complete revision of the savings and loan laws of the State of Texas, which placed savings and loan associations under the control of the Banking Commissioner. Mr. R. B. Cousins, Jr., Chairman of the Board of Insurance Commissioners, writing in the annual report of the Board of Insurance Commissioners for the year 1928, asked the legislature to consider a rewriting of the savings and loan laws,[16] which had not been changed since the original law of 1913.

Senate Bill No. 111 has been amended from time to time since 1929, but it is still the basis of the current law governing savings and loan associations in Texas.[17]

A savings and loan association is defined in Senate Bill No. 111 as:

. . . any association or corporation heretofore or hereafter formed, created or organized which is chartered under any building and loan law, and/or is principally in the business of assisting its members to buy, improve or build homes, or to remove incumbrances therefrom, and which accumulates the funds thus loaned through the issuance or sale of its own shares.[18]

By so defining a savings and loan association, Senate Bill No. 111 places a much narrower limit on the term than did the broadly connotative powers granted to savings and loan associations by the 1913 act.

Sections 2, 3, and 4 of Senate Bill No. 111 greatly increased the power of the Banking Commissioner by giving him greater authority in the approval or rejection of applications for a charter through the following provisions:

Section 2. Commissioner to Investigate.—When any persons shall file a proposed charter or articles of agreement as is elsewhere herein provided, if it appears to the satisfaction of the Banking Commissioner of Texas that the minimum capital

---

[15] General Laws of the State of Texas, Thirty-eighth Legislature, First, Second, and Third Called Sessions, 1923 (Austin, 1923), pp. 108–109.

[16] Fifty-third Annual Report of the Board of Insurance Commissioners, 1928 (Austin, 1928), pp. 205–208.

[17] In some respects it represented a definite departure from the 1913 law.

[18] General Laws of the State of Texas, Forty-first Legislature, Second and Third Called Sessions, 1929 (Austin, no date), p. 100.

required has been paid in cash into the treasury of the association upon subscriptions for shares, the Banking Commissioner of Texas shall ascertain from the best sources at his command, and by such investigation as he may deem necessary, the expense of such investigation to be paid by the incorporators, whether the character, responsibility and general fitness of the persons named in the articles of incorporation are such as to command confidence and warrant belief that the business of the proposed building and loan association will be honestly and efficiently conducted in accordance with the intent and purpose of this Act, and whether the public convenience and advantage will be promoted by allowing such proposed building and loan association to be incorporated and engaged in business, and whether the population in the neighborhood of such place and in the surrounding country affords a reasonable promise of adequate support for the proposed building and loan association. If it shall be satisfied concerning the several matters specified, the Banking Commissioner of Texas shall issue under his official seal a certificate reciting in substance the filing in its office of the articles of incorporation; that such articles conform to all requirements of the law, and that they have been approved, whereupon the persons named in the articles of association, their associates and successors, shall become a corporate body for the period for which they were organized, and shall exercise such powers as are herein granted, and such other powers as are necessary to enable such association to carry out the purpose of its organization, not inconsistent with the provisions of this Act, but before such association shall proceed to do business it shall adopt and have approved by the Banking Commissioner of Texas by-laws for the regulation and management of its business, not inconsistent with the provisions herein provided.

Section 3. Rejection of Application for Charter.—If the Banking Commissioner of Texas shall not be satisfied by such examination that it is expedient and desirable to permit such proposed building and loan association to engage in business, it shall endorse upon each copy of the articles of incorporation the word "refused," with the date of such endorsement, together with the reason for such refusal, and shall forthwith return one copy of such articles of incorporation to the proposed incorporators from whom the same was received, and such refusal shall be conclusive unless the incorporators within thirty days of the issuance of such notice of refusal shall apply to the District Court of Travis County, Texas (which court shall have jurisdiction of such case) for a writ of mandamus to compel the filing of such charter and granting of a permit to do business. Appeals shall lie from the decree of the District Court in the same manner as appeals in other mandamus cases are allowable and taken in this State.

Section 4. Proceed to business—When the Banking Commissioner of Texas shall have approved the organization certificate and the proposed by-laws and shall have issued the certificate of authority to do business, providing that when any building and loan association holding a charter under the laws of this State shall fail to commence business within six months from the date of the issuance of the certificate of authority, such association shall ipso facto be dissolved and its certificate of incorporation shall be null and void, without further executive or judicial action.[19]

The sections quoted above gave the Commissioner authority which has made possible increased effectiveness of state regulation.

[19] *Ibid.*, pp. 100–102.

Section 30 sets forth the requirements which must be met in the organization of a new savings and loan association. Some of these requirements are repeated from the 1913 law, but others have been altered. In full, Section 30 specifies:

Section 30. Articles of Association.—Any number of persons, not less than five, who are citizens of this State, desiring to incorporate a building and loan association may, by complying with the provisions of this Act and entering into articles of association, become a corporate body. Such articles of association shall be signed by the persons associating and acknowledged before some person authorized by the laws of this State to take acknowledgments to deeds, and shall set forth:

1. The name assumed by the association, which shall not be the name assumed by any other association incorporated under this law, nor so similar as to be liable to mislead. The name of the association hereafter formed shall terminate with the words "building and loan association."

2. The purpose for which the association is formed.

3. The name of the city, town or village and the county wherein the principal place of the business of the association is to be located, and which must be within the State of Texas.

4. The amount of its authorized capital stock, which shall be divided into shares of the maturity or par value of not less than one hundred dollars each.

5. The names of the incorporators; their respective occupations and residence address, and a statement of the number of shares subscribed by each, and the amount of cash payment made upon such shares by each.

6. The amount of capital actually paid in which shall in no event be less than one thousand dollars if the home office of the association is located in a town having less than one hundred and fifty thousand inhabitants, and which shall not be less than two thousand dollars if the home office of the association is located in a city having a population of more than ten thousand and less than fifty thousand inhabitants, and which shall not be less than ten thousand dollars if the home office of the association is located in a city having a population of more than fifty thousand and less than one hundred and fifty thousand inhabitants, and which shall not be less than twenty-five thousand dollars if the home office of the association is located in a city having not less than one hundred and fifty thousand inhabitants. The population of all towns and cities for the purpose of fixing the minimum paid-in capital stock of the association under this section shall be ascertained by reference to the last preceding federal census. All payments for shares of required paid-in capital stock must be in lawful money of the United States and must be in the custody of the persons named as the first board of directors.

7. The term of corporate existence which shall not exceed fifty years but which period may be extended as provided in this Act.

8. The number of directors of the association, which shall not be less than five nor more than twenty-one, and the names of the incorporators who shall be its first directors until the first annual meeting. The incorporators named as directors must possess the qualification of directors specified in Section 33 of this Act.[20]

[20] *Ibid.*, pp. 109–110.

In comparing this section with the corresponding section of the 1913 law, certain points are found to be quite different. The first of these is the wise requirement that each newly organized association must include the words "building and loan association" in its title. Elsewhere[21] in this act, others are restricted from using these words in the titles of their businesses.

Senate Bill No. 111 differs from the 1913 law in that it also makes the amount of paid-in capital dependent upon the size of the city in which the association is to be located; this is an attempt to prevent underfinancing.

While the 1913 act did not automatically place all savings and loan associations operating in the state under the control of the act, Senate Bill No. 111 did so by the following provision:

All Texas building and loan associations, now or hereafter organized, and all foreign associations, now or hereafter organized to do business in Texas, shall continue their corporate existence and power and be subject to the provisions of this Act in like manner as corporations which are incorporated hereunder.[22]

Senate Bill No. 111 greatly extended the supervisory powers of the Banking Commissioner from those contained in the 1913 act. Each association was required to file an annual statement with the Commissioner. The statement was to be accompanied by a fee, provided for in Section Nine. The fee might range from a minimum of $50 for an association with assets of less than $250,000 to $550 plus $20 for each $1 million of assets in excess of $6 million.[23] Sections 10, 11, 12, 13, 14, and 15 contain the provisions governing the examinations to be made by the Commissioner of Banking and are reproduced here:

Section 10. Examinations. The Banking Commissioner of Texas shall annually, or oftener if it is deemed advisable, either in person or through duly appointed representatives, make a thorough and complete examination of every building and loan association doing business in this State, and for that purpose shall have the right of access to the offices and to all books and records of said company wherever the same may be kept, and also shall have the right to require the officers, employees or agents of such company, or any person connected therewith, to answer under oath any interrogatories addressed to them pertinent to the business of such company, and any willful false swearing shall be deemed perjury and be punishable as such. The Examiner shall make a report of his findings and file the same in the office of the Banking Commissioner of Texas and the Commissioner shall furnish a copy of such report to the association examined. Such examiner shall report any violation of the law or any unauthorized or unsound practices of such association. He shall be paid such salary or fee for examinations, not to exceed fifteen dollars per day, as shall be authorized by the Banking Commissioner of Texas, which salary or fee and traveling expenses shall be paid out of the fees accumulated under Section 9.

21 *Ibid.*, p. 128.
22 *Ibid.*, p. 109.
23 *Ibid.*, pp. 102–103.

Section 11. Prolonged Audit. The annual fees provided for in Section 9 of this Act entitle each domestic building and loan association to one examination by the Banking Commissioner of Texas, or more if in their judgment additional examinations are necessary or advisable. If in any case the conditions existing in any such association are found to be such as to necessitate, instead of an examination, a prolonged audit and investigation and revaluation of real estate in order to ascertain the true status of its affairs, the whole expense of such examination and re-appraisement shall be defrayed by such association, but the expense of such audit shall not exceed one-fourth of one per cent of the total assets of such association, and in no event shall it exceed one thousand dollars.

Section 12. Accounting System: Appraisal Record. Every association shall keep its books in such form as to accurately show its assets and liabilities, income and disbursements, in detail, and showing the appraised values in ink of the real estate security held in connection with each loan and signed in each case by the appraiser, officer or committee charged with making such estimated valuations.

Section 13. Illegal, Unauthorized, Unsafe, or Fraudulent Practices.—Remedies. In case the Banking Commissioner of Texas shall find, upon examination or from other evidence, that any building and loan association is conducting its business, in whole or in part, contrary to law, or failing to comply with the law, that its assets are less than its liabilities, including all its capital stock, or is conducting its business in an unsafe, unauthorized or fraudulent manner, the Banking Commissioner of Texas shall, by an order in writing addressed to the president of such association, direct attention thereto and order compliance with the law, and that the assets be increased to equal liabilities, and in case such association shall refuse or neglect to comply with any such order lawfully made, or in case any such association is insolvent or in danger of insolvency, or its assets are impaired, then the Banking Commissioner of Texas shall annul its certificate of authority and may begin an action to revoke the charter of such association and for the appointment of a receiver thereof and the winding up of its affairs. Any action begun under this Section shall be brought in the county where such association has its principal place of business, and in the name of the State of Texas on relation of the Banking Commissioner of Texas, and shall be prosecuted by the Attorney General.

Section 14. Report of the Attorney General. Should the Banking Commission of Texas find, upon examination, that the affairs of any such association are in unsound condition and that the interests of the public demand the dissolution of such association and the winding up of its business, it shall so report to the Attorney General, who shall institute the proper proceedings for that purpose.

Section 15. Refusal of any such association to permit the examination of its affairs as authorized by this Act shall be sufficient cause for institution of proceedings to wind up its affairs, and to forfeit the charter and liquidate the association by receivership as permitted by the laws of this state.[24]

As was pointed out earlier in this chapter, the 1913 act did not classify as confidential the information obtained by examiners from the Department of Insurance and Banking. While savings and loan associations were under the supervision of the Commissioner of Insurance, such information was treated as public information and, as such, was available to all who wished

[24] *Ibid.*, pp. 103–105.

to see it. Doubtless, many used this information in making their decisions as to whether or not to withdraw investments from certain associations. It may very well be that the availability of such information aggravated somewhat the runs on savings and loan associations that occurred in Texas during the early months of 1929. Ronald Reynolds states:

In 1929, the Texas statutes were amended placing building and loan associations under the supervision of the Banking Commissioner because for years there had been the practice that the reports of the Commissioner of Insurance were available to the public, while the information of the Banking Commissioner was considered confidential.[25]

Reynolds lists this fact not as one of the reasons but as *the* reason for the transfer of the regulatory function. Regardless of the reasons for so doing, Section 20 of Senate Bill No. 111 was explicit on this point:

Section 20. Disclosures of Examiners—Penalty. Any examiner, inspector, deputy, assistant, or clerk, appointed or acting under the provisions of this Act, failing to keep secret any facts or information adverse to the association obtained in the course of an examination or by reason of his official position, except when the public duty of such officer required him to report upon or take official action regarding the affairs of the association so examined, or who willfully makes a false official report as to the condition of such association, shall be removed from his position or office and shall be fined not more than five hundred dollars, or imprisonment in the county jail for not more than one year, or both. Reports of examinations made to the Banking Commissioner of Texas shall be regarded as confidential and not for public record or inspection, except that for good reason same may be made public by the Commissioner. Nothing herein shall prevent the proper exchange of information relating to building and loan associations and the business thereof with the representatives of building and loan departments of other states, but in no case shall the private business or affairs of any individual association or company be disclosed. Any official violating any provision of this Section, in addition to the penalties herein provided, shall be liable, with his bondsmen, to the person or corporation injured by the disclosure of such secrets; provided, however, that any association shall have a hearing before the Commissioner when dissatisfied with such reports and within thirty days after such hearing and the amending and change, if any, of such report, as may be directed by the Commissioner, such final report shall become a public record open to inspection.[26]

The Annual report to the Governor, provided for in Section 19, becomes public information—as such it may be used by investors. But the reports of the examiners, which supposedly are more revealing, do not.

The fifth called session of the Forty-first Legislature, which convened on February 19, 1930, and adjourned on March 21, amended the 1929 act. The

[25] Ronald Reynolds, *An Analysis of Building and Loan Associations in Texas in 1935.* (MBA thesis, The University of Texas, Austin, 1937), p. 1.

[26] *General Laws of the State of Texas, Firty-first Legislature, Second and Third Called Sessions* (Austin, no date), p. 106.

amendment applied only to Section 40 and provided that if an association were in the process of voluntary or involuntary liquidation, the borrower's net share holdings would be offset against his loan.[27] Aside from this minor change, the Forty-first Legislature did not alter the 1929 act.

The regular session of the Forty-second Legislature, which convened on January 19, 1931, and adjourned on May 23, 1931, passed Senate Bill No. 332, which made a slight change in Section 11 of the 1929 act. Section 11 originally provided that while the expense of a prolonged audit was to be borne by the savings and loan association being examined, the total expense could not exceed one-fourth of one percent of the total assets or one thousand dollars. Senate Bill No. 332 removed this limitation on the cost of a prolonged audit which was to be paid by the association.[28]

The regular session of the Forty-second Legislature also passed House Bill No. 12, which was approved on March 24, 1931. This bill amended Section 33, which originally provided that the amount of stock a shareholder was required to own to be eligible for directorship depended upon the location of the association. While House Bill No. 12 did not repeal this provision, it modified it somewhat by inserting the following provison:

Provided, however, any person who is the owner in good faith and in his own right on the books of the association shares upon which Two Hundred ($200.00) Dollars in cash has been paid, shall be eligible to election as a director in an association having assets of less than Three Hundred Fifty Thousand ($350,000.00) Dollars, regardless of the location of the association, and such amount shall not be reduced by withdrawal or pledge for a loan with the association, or in any other manner so long as he remains a director of the association.[29]

Senate Bill No. 553 extended the powers of the Banking Commissioner in case of voluntary liquidation by amending Section 56 with the following provision:

Provided, however, that the plan of the liquidation, including contemplated expenses and the sale of any or all of its assets shall have the approval of the Banking Commissioner or his authorized representative before any expenses are incurred or any sale or sales are made, and any and all expenses incurred by the Banking Commissioner or his duly authorized representative shall be paid from the assets of the Association.[30]

The third called session of the Forty-second Legislature passed Senate Bills 8 and 9, which amended several sections of the savings and loan acts and added two new sections. One of these, Section 78a, provided that:

[27] *General Laws of the State of Texas, Forty-first Legislature, Fourth and Fifth Called Sessions* (Austin, no date), pp. 193–194.
[28] *General Laws of the State of Texas, Forty-second Legislature, 1933* (n.p.), p. 320.
[29] *Ibid.*, pp. 53–54.
[30] *Ibid.*, p. 332.

. . . any building and loan association, savings and loan association, cooperative bank, homestead association, insurance company, Fraternal Benefit Association, and Societies, or savings bank or any Loan Company organized under the provisions of Chapter 275 of the Acts of the Regular Session of the 40th Legislature, now organized or hereafter to be organized, which is eligible to become a member of the Federal Home Loan Bank, in compliance with the provisions of the Act of Congress known and cited as the "Federal Home Loan Bank Act" shall be and is hereby fully authorized and empowered to subscribe for the stock of the Home Loan Bank for the district in which it is located, and to invest its funds in such stock, for the purpose and to the extent required by the provisions of the Federal Home Loan Bank Act for the qualification of members therein.[31]

A second entirely new section, Section 21a, subsequently changed to Section 22a, was added at this time. Section 21a provided that:

Any building and loan association heretofore or hereafter organized under the laws of this State shall have the power in any special meeting called for that purpose, to reorganize the association and provide for the future transaction of its future business under the provisions of this Act by a vote of two-thirds of the shares of the members of this association who vote at such meeting . . .[32]

The Banking Commissioner was given the power to supervise all phases of the reorganization, and the privilege of reorganizing was extended to associations in the process of voluntary or involuntary liquidation. Heretofore, if an association became insolvent, it was liquidated, either voluntary or involuntarily. This provision permitted an association to reorganize under the same or a different name and to:

. . . provide for the exchange of shares in the association for shares of the same or different class in the reorganized association, and may fix the time or times prior to which notice of withdrawal of such shares so issued in exchange for shares in the association being reorganized shall not be given. . . .[33]

Truly this was a depression measure; it afforded relief to associations faced with liquidation.

Senate Bill No. 9 amended Section 27 by greatly increasing the rights of an association to hold, manage, and dispose of foreclosed real property. Section 44, which regulated borrowing by savings and loan associations, was amended to provide:

. . . that any loans made by such Association from the Federal Home Loan Bank or from the Reconstruction Finance Corporation or from any other corporation or agency established under authority of the United States Government (except National Banks) may be consummated by such association without obtaining the approval of the Banking Commissioner regardless of the restrictions fixed by this

[31] *General and Special Laws of the State of Texas, Forty-second Legislature, Third Called Session, 1932* (n.p.), pp. 31–32.
[32] *Ibid.*, p. 35.
[33] *Ibid.*, p. 36.

Act. No loan, except such as may be made from the Federal Home Loan Bank or from the Reconstruction Finance Corporation or similar Federal agency, shall be made for a longer period than two years. Associations are authorized and empowered to assign and pledge its notes, mortgages or other property, and to repledge the shares of stock pledged as collateral security (without securing the consent of the owner thereto) as security for the repayment of its indebtedness due to an association, shall have the right to enforce, in his own name or in the name of the Association, all appropriate remedies to enforce collection, whether or not the stock described in connection with said note be held by such pledgee or holder. Any obligation incurred or loan made by an association shall constitute a claim against the corporate assets, and shall be payable in advance of, and by preference over, all claims or rights of the shareholders in any assets of said association, and shall prime and outrank particularly any demand or application for the withdrawal or cancellation of all classes of shares in said association.[34]

Section 47, which provided for large withdrawals, was greatly altered. Originally, associations were permitted to require prior notice of intent to withdraw funds in amounts greater than $500. Senate Bill No. 9 reduced this figure to $100. The act originally provided that in the event that demands for withdrawals had not been met in 12 months, all net receipts were to be used to meet withdrawal demands; this was changed to provide:

Notwithstanding the existence of a withdrawal list, the board of directors, as long as there are debts owing by the Association, may use all or any part of the funds and current receipts for the payment of such debts; provided, however, that after allowance for due and past due indebtedness of the Association, one-half of the "net receipts" of the Association in any one month shall be applied to the payment of withdrawals and maturities when there are maturities or requests for withdrawals on file.

After filing notices of withdrawal provided herein, the withdrawing member shall be entitled, if so provided in the by-laws, to the dividends credited to the same class of shares until the final payment of his shares is made, and membership in the association shall remain unimpaired so long as any accumulation remains to his credit. The existence of a withdrawal list shall not prevent the making of new loans to new or continuing members, and the board of directors, in its discretion, may borrow money to be used solely for the purpose of making mortgage loans to the members of the Association, in which event all of such amount of borrowed money may be exclusively used for the purpose borrowed.

The by-laws and all certificates of shares of stock in any building and loan association operating under the provisions of this title shall expressly provide that withdrawals of subscriptions or funds in said Association shall be paid only as and when funds are available out of receipts and income for the purpose. Such Association shall not hold out as an inducement to the public or members thereof to purchase share or shares of such stock that such funds may be withdrawn at a time certain upon notice of the shareholders' intention to withdraw such funds.[35]

Section 48, which defined withdrawal value, was amended to allow that:

[34] *Ibid.*, p. 41.
[35] *Ibid.*, pp. 41–43.

. . . a reasonable portion of the dividends previously credited to the shares or of the earnings previously allocated to the shares, upon cancellation and withdrawal of such shares before maturity, may be retained by the Association and deducted from the withdrawal value of the shares, if the by-laws of the Association definitely so provide.[36]

The Forty-third Legislature did not specifically amend the savings and loan laws, but it did pass Senate Bill No. 561, which provided that several financial institutions—among them savings and loan associations—might invest in:

. . . all bonds, debentures, notes, collateral trust certificates, and other such evidences of indebtedness, which have been, or which may be issued, by Federal Home Loan Bank Board, or Home Owners Loan Corporation, or by any Federal Savings and Loan Association, or by the Reconstruction Finance Corporation or by the Federal Land Bank, or by any entity, corporation, or agency which has been or which may be created by or authorized by any act which has been created, or which may hereafter be enacted, by the Congress of the United States, or by any amendment thereto, which has for its purpose the relief of, refinancing of, or assistance to owners of mortgaged, or encumbered homes, farms, and other real estate.[37]

The Forty-fourth Legislature amended several sections of the savings and loan code in order to recognize and make provisions for federal associations and to permit associations to handle loans insured under the Federal Housing Act. Senate Bill No. 97, approved on April 6, 1935, again amended Section 21a, which deals with reorganizations. This amendment allowed reorganization as either a state or a federal association and also allowed the creation of a second association to hold a part of the assets of the original association.[38] This section was to be used often in the next few years. The usual procedure was to create a new organization to hold the preferred assets and to use the old association as a liquidating device.

Section 38, which regulates the investments which a savings and loan association may make, was amended to permit real estate loans of 75 percent of value—the banking commissioner had the right to reduce this to 66 percent. Loans insured under the Federal Housing Act were exempted from this requirement.[39]

Section 55, which provides for consolidation, was amended to permit state associations to consolidate with federal associations.[40] Section 55a, was added by Senate Bill No. 97. It provided that:

Any building and loan association chartered and operating under the laws of the State of Texas, by whatever name or style it may be designated, eligible to be-

[36] Ibid., p. 43.
[37] General Laws of the State of Texas, Forty-third Legislature, 1933 (n.p.), p. 406.
[38] General and Special Laws of the State of Texas, Forty-fourth Legislature, 1935 (n.p.), pp. 159–161.
[39] Ibid., pp. 162–166.
[40] Ibid., p. 167.

come a Federal Savings and Loan Association under any Federal Act, may convert itself into a Federal Savings and Loan Association by following the procedure here-under outlined.[41]

The requirements for conversion include a two-thirds affirmative vote of all the shares, to be voted at a special meeting called for this purpose. There was also a provision for conversion from a federal association to a state one.

The Forty-sixth Legislature passed three bills amending the savings and loan code: Senate Bills No.'s 13, 115, and 191. Senate Bill No. 115 made only a minor change in the bonding requirement of employees, officers, and others. Senate Bill No. 191 made a slight change in the regulation of foreign associations operating within the state. Senate Bill No. 13, however, amended the code at several points. It provided for a savings and loan super-visor, by amending Section 7 to read in part:

The Banking Commissioner shall appoint a supervisor who has at least two years' actual experience as manager-executive of a building and loan association, or shall have not less than (18) months actual experience as a supervisor of a building and loan association, or who has had at least (2) years' experience in the employ of a building and loan association, and not less than (2) years' actual experience as an examiner.[42]

Section 10a was added at this time and provided that the State could accept the examination report of a Federal Home Loan Bank or the Federal Savings and Loan Insurance Corporation in lieu of an examination of its own.[43]

Section 16, which provides for the procedure to be followed in liquidating an association which is found on examination to warrant liquidation or an association which refuses to permit an examination, was amended to list in detail the procedures for such a liquidation.[44]

Sections 23, 24, and 25, which regulate the status of shares owned by married women and minors, joint owners, and trust funds, respectively, were amended to give savings and loan association shares essentially the same status as savings accounts in commercial banks.[45]

Section 28, which prohibited savings and loan associations from accepting deposits, was amended to permit the acceptance of "money from members to be used for the purpose of paying taxes, assessments, and in-surance premiums on the property on which the association has a lien."[46]

Section 30 was amended to permit the use of the term "savings and loan association" instead of "building and loan association."[47]

[41] *Ibid.*
[42] *General Laws of the State of Texas, Forty-sixth Legislature, 1939* (n.p.), pp. 76–77.
[43] *Ibid.*
[44] *Ibid.*, pp. 77–78.
[45] *Ibid.*, pp. 79–80.
[46] *Ibid.*, pp. 80–81.
[47] *Ibid.*, p. 81.

Section 35 was amended to permit a "person, firm, co-partnership, association or corporation" to be a member and to have voting rights. It also provided that borrowers be allowed to vote. This section also permitted an association to accept as security the accounts of a member other than the borrower on a real estate or other loan.[48]

Sections 38a and 38b were added by Senate Bill 13. Section 38a permitted 90 percent loans secured by shares or insured by the Federal Housing Administration.[49] Section 38b approved the action taken by some associations in obtaining share insurance under the provisions of the National Housing Act of 1934 and authorized other associations to obtain insurance, and it designated such associations as "insured associations."[50]

Section 42, which provided for dividend and reserve practices, was amended to increase the contribution to a reserve account from 1 percent to 5 percent by providing:

If the reserve fund shall not equal five (5) per cent of the capital at the time of each apportionment of profits, hereinafter provided, the directors shall, before apportioning profits, set aside, as a reserve fund, not less than five (5) per cent of the net profits accruing since last prior apportionment, and shall continue to do so until said fund shall amount to at least five (5) per cent of the capital of the association. Said reserve fund shall at all times be available to meet losses arising from any source, including depreciation of securities.

The reserve fund of not less than five (5) per cent of the net profits accruing since last prior apportionment herein required to be provided may be considered identical with, and not supplemental to, the reserves required to be set up by insured associations by the Federal Savings and Loan Insurance Corporation.[51]

Section 42 also set forth the practice to be followed in paying dividends.

The Forty-seventh Legislature, which convened on January 14, 1941, and adjourned on July 3, made only slight changes in the savings and loan laws. Senate Bill No. 208 added Section 38c, which provided for lending in "defense housing areas" and for certain repair and improvement loans.[52] This legislature also passed Senate Bill No. 61, which changed Section 49, the section which treated matured shares. Prior to this date, associations were required to notify purchasers of instalment shares when they matured and the shares could be withdrawn. However, there was no provision as to what would be done in the event they were not withdrawn. This amendment removed the requirement that the association notify the purchaser and pro-

[48] *Ibid.*, pp. 82–83.
[49] *Ibid.*, p. 85.
[50] *Ibid.*, pp. 85–86.
[51] *Ibid.*, p. 86.
[52] *General and Special Laws of the State of Texas, Forty-seventh Legislature, 1941* (n.p.), p. 347.

vided that if such shares were not withdrawn, they were to be treated as "fully paid shares."[53]

The regular session of the Forty-eighth Legislature, in session from January 12 to May 11, 1943, passed Senate Bill No. 61. This act made several slight changes in the laws affecting savings and loan associations. Section 7 was amended to permit the Federal Home Loan Bank and the Federal Savings and Loan Insurance Corporation to examine state member or insured associations and to permit member associations to act as fiscal agents for the United States government.[54]

Section 30 was changed by adding:

. . . and associations authorized by their articles of incorporation or by-laws to issue Permanent Reserve Fund Stock, may provide in their articles of incorporation or by-laws that all or at least a majority of the Board of Directors shall be elected from the shareholders holding Permanent Reserve Fund Stock.[55]

Of all the legislation relating to savings and loan associations passed by this legislature, this is doubtless the most significant, for it increased the ease with which permanent stockholders could maintain control of the association.

Section 37 provided that the amount of permanent stock must equal 5 percent of the gross assets of an association or $250,000, whichever is the smaller. This amendment lowered the required proportion to 3 percent.[56]

Senate Bill No. 61 also amended Section 40 to fix the maximum prepayment penalty at 5 percent of the amount of the anticipatory payment,[57] and it amended Section 73, the section dealing with failure to comply with the law, by empowering the Attorney General to bring suit to collect any penalty.[58]

The Forty-ninth Legislature passed two bills that amended savings and loan laws. Senate Bill No. 8 amended Section 30 to allow the use of the terms "savings association," and "savings institution"[59] in the title of an association. Heretofore they had been referred to as "savings and loan" or "building and loan associations." Senate Bill No. 7, approved on March 5, 1945, permitted state associations to make loans under the "G. I. Bill" by amending Section 38a to read:

Any building and loan association organized under the laws of this state may make loans pursuant to the provisions of Sections 500, 501, 504 and 505 of Chap-

[53] *Ibid.*, p. 482.

[54] *General and Special Laws of the State of Texas, Forty-eighth Legislature, 1943* (n.p.), p. 483.

[55] *Ibid.*, p. 485.

[56] *Ibid.*, p. 486.

[57] *Ibid.*, p. 493.

[58] *Ibid.*

[59] *General and Special Laws of the State of Texas, Forty-ninth Legislature, 1945* (n.p.), pp. 66–67.

ter V, Title III of the Act of Congress, entitled "Servicemen's Readjustment Act of 1944," approved by the President on June 22, 1944, and all amendments thereto, as well as any and all regulations that may be hereafter promulgated under the provisions of said sections of said Act of Congress. Such building and loan associations are authorized and empowered to contract for, and obtain such insurance or guaranty of the payment of such loans, advancements or investments as may be provided in such sections of such Act or any amendments thereto, or under any regulations promulgated thereunder. Such building and loan associations may invest any of their funds, in such loans, credits or obligations without limitation as to amount loaned to any one borrower, or period of maturity, under the provisions of Section 500, 501, 504 and 505 of Chapter V, Title III of said Act of Congress, and under all amendments thereto, as well as under any and all regulations that have been heretofore promulgated or that may be hereafter promulgated under the provisions of said Sections of said Act of Congress.[60]

The Fiftieth Legislature, which convened on January 14, 1947, and adjourned on June 6, made only two slight changes in savings and loan legislation. Senate Bill No. 14 provided that the number of directors, within the statutory limitations provided (at least five but not more than twenty-one), could be changed without an amendment to the charter by a vote of the stockholders at any regular or special meeting.[61] This legislature also passed Senate Bill No. 15, which amended Section 54 and stated the manner in which property owned by an association was to be rendered for taxation. The effect of this amendment was to clarify rather than to change greatly the method in which such property was rendered. As amended, the section required:

Each building and loan association incorporated under the laws of Texas and Federal savings and loan associations domiciled in this State, shall hereafter be required to render for state, county and municipal taxation, all of its real estate as other real estate is rendered. The personal property of each such building and loan association shall be valued as other personal property is valued for assessment in this State, and shall be rendered by such association in the following manner:

1. Each such association shall render for state, county and municipal taxation in the city and in the county where its home office is located, its office furniture and fixtures;

2. From the total valuation of each such association's entire assets shall be deducted the following:

(a) All the debts of every kind and character owed by such association;

(b) All tax free securities owned by such association;

(c) The book value of all its shares outstanding;

(d) The reserves and undivided profits authorized by law;

(e) The assessed value of its furniture and fixtures;

---

[60] *Ibid.*, p. 284.

[61] *General and Special Laws of the State of Texas, Fiftieth legislature, 1947* (n.p.), p. 348.

(f) The assessed value of all real estate owned by the association; and the remainder, if any there be, shall be taxable as personal property against each such association.[62]

The Fifty-first Legislature, which met from January 11 to July 6, 1949, passed four bills pertaining to savings and loan associations. Senate Bill No. 30 gave the board of directors of a savings and loan association the power to close the association on any day or days it chose. There had been some question as to whether or not a savings and loan association had the right to close on a "banking day." This amendment gave them the right to do so.[63]

Senate Bill No. 31 prohibited associations from charging a membership, cancellation, or withdrawal fee by providing that:

It shall be unlawful for any building and loan association organized under the laws of this State, or any building and loan association authorized to do business in this State under a permit, to charge investing members a membership fee, cancellation fee or withdrawal fee.

Any building and loan association organized under the laws of this State, or any building and loan association authorized to do business in this State, which violates any of the provisions of this Section, then and in that event, the Banking Commissioner of Texas shall annul its certificate of authority and may begin an action to revoke the charter of such building and loan association and for the appointment of a receiver thereof and the winding up of its affairs. Any action begun under this Section shall be brought in Travis County, Texas, and in the name of the State of Texas on relation of the Banking Commissioner of Texas and shall be prosecuted by the Attorney General.[64]

Senate Bill No. 33 amended three sections of the laws relating to savings and loan associations. The amendment to Section 25, the section dealing with trust-fund investments, was a minor one; it required an order of a probate court before certain investments could be accepted.[65] The second change, which appeared in Section 26, permitted construction loans by the following amendment:

. . . any building and loan association may make construction or temporary loans upon real estate security to any one person where the amount of the loan to one borrower does not exceed four per cent of the entire assets of such association, or where such loan does not exceed fifty per cent of the reserves and undivided profits of such association, whichever is the least.[66]

The third amendment in Senate Bill No. 33, found in Section 38, affects investments. Originally associations were required to limit loans secured by

---

[62] *Ibid.*, p. 349.

[63] *General and Special Laws of the State of Texas, Fifty-first Legislature, 1949* (n.p.), p. 695.

[64] *Ibid.*, pp. 696–697.

[65] *Ibid.*, p. 966.

[66] *Ibid.*, p. 967.

pledged shares that the borrower was currently purchasing to $300 if the association had total assets of less than $1,000,000, or to $1,000 if the assets exceeded $1,000,000. This amendment raised these limits to $500 and $1,500, respectively.[67] The maximum maturity was also increased from eighteen to forty-eight months.[68]

Senate Bill No. 260, the fourth bill dealing with savings and loan associations, amended the sections pertaining to the examination and collection of fees from foreign savings and loan associations and also increased the maximum pay of savings and loan examiners from $15 to $30 a day.[69]

The Fifty-second Legislature passed two bills which amended the laws under which savings and loan associations operate; these were House Bills 51 and 104. House Bill No. 51 was not specifically a savings and loan bill but applied to the entire Banking Department. It amended Section 9 by providing that all fees collected from savings and loan associations, along with other fees collected by the Banking Department, "shall be retained by said Department and shall be expended only for the expenses of such Department."[70] The second bill, House Bill No. 104, amended Section 8 to require monthly reports from state associations in addition to the annual reports already required.[71]

The Fifty-third Legislature, which convened on January 13, 1953, and adjourned on May 27, passed only one bill, House Bill No. 135, which related to savings and loan associations. This bill amended Section 24, the section pertaining to joint accounts, by providing:

A married woman or a minor is authorized to enter into, fulfill, and receive the benefits of contracts for such joint accounts, as if such married woman was a feme sole, or as if such minor was of legal age, provided, however, that where share or share accounts are issued in the name of two (2) or more persons or the survivors of either, and the survivor is a minor, the proceeds of the joint account shall be paid to his legally appointed and qualified guardian.[72]

[67] *Ibid.*, p. 969.
[68] The significance of this amendment is that it makes it possible for savings and loan associations to engage in "personal" finance activities on a much broader scale.
[69] *Op. cit.*, p. 487.
[70] *General and Special Laws of the State of Texas, Fifty-second Legislature, 1951* (n.p.), p. 204.
[71] *Ibid.*, p. 203.
[72] *General and Special Laws of the State of Texas, Fifty-third Legislature, 1953* (n.p.), p. 1028.

CHAPTER V

Savings and Loan Associations in Texas, 1916–1936

Savings and loan associations in Texas were placed under the supervision of the Commissioner of Insurance and Banking in 1913. The legislation passed in that year has been discussed in some detail in Chapter IV. In order to facilitate discussion of savings and loan activity in Texas from 1916 through 1936, this book divides the era into two periods: the first extends from 1916 through 1929 and roughly approximates the first period of extensive growth of the industry within the state. The second period includes the years from 1930 through 1936, a period of contraction within the savings and loan industry of Texas.

The Period 1916–1929

Savings and loan associations operating in Texas were required in 1913 to register with, and submit reports to, the Commissioner of Insurance and Banking; however, these associations are not mentioned in the annual reports of the Commissioner of Insurance and Banking until 1916.[1]

The annual reports of the Commissioners of Insurance and Banking for the years 1916 through 1921 contained statistics on savings and loan associations, but the associations were not mentioned in the texts of the reports until 1922. Presumably savings and loan associations did not constitute an important enough segment of the financial institutions in Texas to warrant special or individual mention. In the *Forty-seventh Annual Report of the Commissioner of Insurance and Banking*, Ed Hall, the retiring commissioner, stated:

Mutual building and loan associations, under the laws of this State, are chartered by the Secretary of State and then placed under the supervision of this Department. There has been very little activity along this line, since the law was enacted in 1914, until recently. However, during the year 1921, twenty-seven of these associations have been formed and twenty-eight to date this year, there being in operation, at this time, eighty-eight.[2]

[1] Apparently no associations submitted reports to the Department of Insurance and Banking until 1916, for Mr. R. B. Cousins, Chairman, Board of Insurance Commissioners in 1928, made a study of the early records of his department and could find no information relating to savings and loan associations in Texas before 1916.

[2] *Forty-seventh Annual Report of the Commissioner of Insurance and Banking, 1922* (Austin), p. 6.

As can be seen by reference to Tables 7 and 8, the savings and loan industry grew slowly until after the depression of 1921. By 1922, however, the rapid increase in the number of associations, which was to reach a high of 176 in 1929, had begun. This growth presented certain problems of regulation. While the associations were under supervision of the Commissioner of Insurance and Banking, they were actually receiving very little supervision. The legislature failed to appropriate adequately for this purpose. Mr. Hall, in the report referred to previously, stated:

. . . Very little supervision has been exercised in the past and very little will be in the future, unless sufficient appropriation is made to carry out the intent of the law. The law is indefinite in a great many respects and has never in any of the phases, been adjudicated by our courts, which makes administration on doubtful points very unsatisfactory.[3]

And he warned that:

Unless something is done, at an early date, for closer supervision, as well as clarifying the law, I feel that before long many unsatisfactory situations will arise which will destroy the usefulness of what is otherwise a good law.[4]

The legislature did not, however, follow Mr. Hall's recommendation. For the next two years (1923–24) the associations received very little supervision. Mr. Hall resigned his post on January 20, 1923, and J. L. Chapman was appointed to serve the remaining eight months of the unexpired term. A Mr. Scott held the position of Commissioner of Insurance from August 14, 1923, until September 30, 1925.[5] In the three annual reports of the Commissioner of Insurance issued under his direction, the problems of savings and loan associations were not mentioned. Apparently they continued to receive little if any attention from the regulatory agency. Mr. Scott did not comment upon a lack of funds.

R. L. Daniel became Commissioner of Insurance on September 1, 1925, and in the 1926 report, the first annual report published under his direction, he expressed great concern over the status of the savings and loan industry. He found supervision lacking in the following important respects: (1) the legislature did not make adequate appropriations to pay for examinations; (2) inasmuch as the worth of a large part of the assets of an association—real estate loans—depends upon the value of the properties pledged as security, an examination cannot be valid unless the examiner is able to hire competent appraisers, and there was no provision for this; and (3) the Commissioner did not have power to prevent the organization of associations that, in his opinion, should not be organized.

[3] *Ibid.*, pp. 6–7.
[4] *Ibid.*, p. 7.
[5] As was explained in Chapter IV, the Department of Insurance and Banking was divided into two separate departments in 1923.

On the first point mentioned above, Mr. Daniel stated:

The appropriations made by former legislatures have not been sufficient to enable
the department to give the building and loan associations such supervision and
make such examinations as the law contemplates and the business itself deserves.
. . . The Regular Session of the Thirty-Ninth Legislature appropriated $3,000.00
per year for this purpose and provided that none of this amount should be used
for traveling expenses. It is impossible to secure a competent examiner for $8.00
per day. A competent examiner can be secured for no less than $115.00 [he ob-
viously means $15.00] per day and all traveling expenses. Examiners of insurance
and trust companies command even better pay. This situation was presented to the
State Building and Loan League soon after I came into office and the members of
the League, by voluntary assessment, raised a fund of $4,405.00 for the purpose
of supplementing the appropriation made by the Legislature. . . . Owing to the
lack of funds during the first few months of the year, we have not been able to
complete the work as it should be and as the law contemplates. We are now con-
fronted with the same condition we had last year and, unless the State Building
and Loan League again comes to our rescue, during the coming year we are going
to be unable to examine these associations as the law contemplates and proper
supervision demands.[6]

In regard to determination of the need for a proposed association the Commissioner stated:

I am of the opinion that the law should be amended so as to give the Commissioner authority, and make it his duty to make the necessary investigations in
order to determine whether or not there is a demand or necessity for the estab-
lishment of a building and loan association in any locality before a permit is
issued for the operation of such an association in that locality. . . .[7]

Had this provision been granted to the Commissioner, and had he exercised discretion in the granting of additional charters, doubtless much of
the distress of the depression which followed could have been avoided.
While "free" chartering of savings and loan associations does appeal to
would-be organizers, and while it may have a democratic aspect, there is no
denying that it does not make for strength in financial businesses. Actually,
supervisory authorities in the savings and loan field have not, even today,
accepted the principle of limiting the number of institutions to the extent
that the banking industry has.

Mr. Daniel discussed the other shortcomings of the existing law and noted
that:

. . . The Commissioner should also be clothed with authority to investigate and
pass upon the business ability and integrity of the organizers and officers of building and loan associations and for just cause, require the resignation of any in-

[6] *Fifty-first Annual Report of the Commissioner of Insurance, 1926* (Austin, 1926),
pp. 5–6.
[7] *Ibid.*, p. 6.

competent or dishonest person from the management of such an association or refuse a permit to any association until satisfied of the honesty and integrity of the
officers and directors of such concern. Building and loan associations are started
without funds on the part of the organizers and promoters. The money they collect usually comes from the savings of people who toil and have a desire to ac-
cumulate funds with which to buy homes for themselves and their families and the
law should not permit unscrupulous or incompetent persons to organize or operate
associations and handle the funds of these people, who, as a rule, have no time
or opportunity to investigate the situation themselves; they rely upon the fact
that the association in licensed by, and is under the supervision of the Department
of Insurance as a protection of their funds. At the same time, they are unaware of
the fact that the Department is without sufficient funds with which to properly
supervise the association and that the Commissioner is not clothed with the power
to prevent incompetent or dishonest persons from engaging in the building and
loan business.[8]

This request was discussed in Chapter IV. By all means, the regulatory
agency should have the power to prevent the organization of associations
which do not have a reasonably good chance of success.

The number of associations continued to increase with alarming speed,
but the legislature failed to keep pace by appropriating adequate funds for
their supervision. The appropriation for the year ending on August 31,
1927, amounted to only $3,000, even though the number of associations had
increased to 144. Less than $21.00 was allowed for each association to be
examined. Again the League came to the aid of the associations and appropriated over $4,500 to pay for supervision. In the *Fifty-second Annual
Report of the Commissioner of Insurance of Texas*, Mr. R. L. Daniel again
commented on the need for additional funds:

It is quite evident that a proper supervision and examination of building and
loan associations of Texas cannot be accomplished with less than about $8,500. We
would respectfully suggest, therefore, that if the Legislatures in their appropriations desire to economize that they exercise this economy somewhere else rather
than deny a proper supervision of building and loan associations and endanger
the savings of our citizens.[9]

Mr. Daniel's somewhat caustic advice to the legislature apparently fell
upon deaf ears, for adequate appropriations were not forthcoming for some
time. Too, Mr. Daniel was leaving the office of Commissioner and was succeeded by R. B. Cousins, whose opinion of the situation was somewhat different. Mr. Cousins in the first report prepared under his supervision, dated
May 19, 1928, stated:

. . . We think it has been too often true in the past, although, of course, not in-
variably true, that the examiners who have represented the department have not

[8] *Ibid.*, pp. 6–7.
[9] *Fifty-second Annual Report of the Commissioner of Insurance, 1927* (Austin, 1927),
pp. 5–6.

completely understood the responsibility of their position. It seems also that the Legislature has not had its attention brought to the necessity for supervision of these associations nor the requirements for efficient examination.[10]

It is somewhat difficult to reconcile Mr. Cousin's comments with the strong language used by his immediate predecessor in calling the attention of the legislature to the need of greater appropriations.

Mr. Cousins did, however, note some serious dangers in the supervision given to savings and loan associations. Particularly, he feared that the valuation of property upon which loans were being made was excessive. He urged caution in appraising, and inasmuch as he seemingly did not view the situation with alarm, this doubtless was a rather severe warning.

For the most part, Mr. Cousins, writing in 1928, was pleased with the status of the industry. He said:

> While this enormous increase in volume of business is a matter of considerable interest, we think it much more important that only one association operating under the building and loan law of this State has been liquidated through a receivership, with a loss to investors, and the reports which we have of the associations now doing business indicate that there is not a single association in Texas in danger of insolvency. This may be taken as a testimonial to the strength of the collateral on which the assets of these associations are based.[11]

While the statement that "not a single association in Texas" is in danger of insolvency is a rash statement at any time, it proved to be especially so in 1928. Shortly after the appearance of the report referred to above, the industry found itself in the beginning of a long and trying period of depression.

In 1929 the legislature passed Senate Bill 111, discussed in Chapter IV. This bill transferred control of savings and loan associations to the Banking Commissioner and gave the Commissioner many of the powers requested by Insurance Commissioner Daniels. The transfer seems to have been a wise one. While the Insurance Commissioner can hardly be blamed for practices that resulted from lack of appropriations and legal authority, savings and loan associations have increasingly come to resemble banks and to require a type of examination similar to that applied to banks. For better or worse, shares in savings associations have taken on many of the characteristics of time deposits in commercial banks.

One of the alleged reasons for the transfer of savings and loan supervision from the Commissioner of Insurance to the Commissioner of Banking was that the information obtained by the Insurance Department was classified as "public" information and as such was available to all who wanted to see

[10] *Fifty-third Annual Report of the Board of Insurance Commissioners, 1928* (Austin, 1928), p. 206.
[11] *Ibid.*

it. This information included reports of examinations and audits. While it might be desirable for an investor to be able to see the examination report of an association in which he had an investment, the availability of such information, particularly when used by those who were not familiar with such examinations, could contribute to a feeling of uncertainty and aggravate if not cause distress in the industry. I. Friedlander is generally credited with having promoted the 1929 law which, with amendments, constitutes the present code governing savings and loan activity within the state. The 1929 law, as can be seen in Chapter IV, provided many sorely needed changes in the 1913 act as amended and resulted in closer and more effective supervision of the industry.

This period, from 1916 to 1929, also saw great changes in the type of operation in the savings and loan field. In 1916 the Continental Savings and Building Association of Dallas was organized. This was the first Texas association to "grasp the possibilities of large-scale development inherent in the permanent plan."[12] Before 1916 the associations were mostly small ones. In 1917 balance sheets for each association were first published in the annual report. In that year, of the twenty-nine associations operating in the state, none had assets of as much as $350,000; only three had assets in excess of $250,000; eight had assets in excess of $100,000; and five had assets of less than $10,000. By 1929 the size of associations had increased substantially; twenty-five domestic associations had assets in excess of $1,000,000.

Another development which occurred during the 1920's and which was to affect greatly the structure of the savings and loan industry in Texas was that of the permanent stock plan. This plan, discussed in some detail in Chapter II, had the effect of giving the owners of permanent stock essentially the same rights and control powers as those enjoyed by owners of common stock in other corporations. Maco Stewart, who became president of the Guarantee Building and Loan Company of Galveston, is given credit for introducing the permanent stock plan to Texas.

The period from 1916 through 1929 was one of great activity in the formation and dissolution of associations. During this period 254 new associations were chartered, and 110 of these went out of business through liquidation or forfeiture of charter, or else consolidated with other associations.

Another change which occurred during the period from 1916 through 1929 was the increase in relative importance of Texas associations as compared to foreign associations.[13] On December 31, 1917, the combined assets of all Texas savings and loan associations amounted to $2,336,832, and the

---

[12] H. Morton Bodfish (ed.), *History of Building and Loan in the United States* (Chicago: United States Building and Loan League, 1931), p. 580.

[13] A foreign association is one chartered in a state other than Texas.

TABLE 7

SAVINGS AND LOAN ASSOCIATIONS IN TEXAS, 1916 TO 1929

Year	State associations	Foreign associations	Total associations
1916	27	1	28
1917	29	1	30
1918	25	1	26
1919	31	3	34
1920	40	4	44
1921	59	4	63
1922	82	4	86
1923	89	4	93
1924	102	4	106
1925	119	4	123
1926	129	4	133
1927	144	5	149
1928	162	5	167
1929	176	6	182

Sources: Annual Reports of the Commissioner of Insurance and Banking, 1916–1922; Annual Reports of the Commissioner of Insurance, 1923–1928; *First Annual Report of Building and Loan Associations, 1929.*

TABLE 8

ASSETS OF SAVINGS AND LOAN ASSOCIATIONS IN TEXAS, 1916 TO 1929

Year	Total assets of domestic associations (*thousands of dollars*)	Total assets of foreign associations (*thousands of dollars*)
1916	1,855	3,307
1917	2,336	3,432
1918	2,484	3,863
1919	3,251	13,888
1920	4,464	17,313
1921	7,163	19,699
1922	12,036	24,330
1923	21,060	31,781
1924	33,998	39,570
1925	48,983	40,053
1926	71,755	50,759
1927	92,654	61,289
1928	113,034	n.a.
1929	137,016	89,306

Sources: Annual Reports of the Commissioner of Insurance and Banking, 1916–1922; Annual Reports of the Commissioner of Insurance, 1923–1928; *First Annual Report of Building and Loan Associations, 1929.*

assets of the one foreign association doing business in the state totaled $3,432,472. It was not until 1925 that total assets of Texas savings and loan associations exceeded those of foreign associations. Table 8 lists the total assets of both Texas and foreign associations during this period. Since 1925 the savings and loan industry in Texas has been dominated by local associations. Even before this date, the local associations conducted most of the business, for the total assets of foreign associations does not refer only to the portion of their assets in Texas.

TABLE 9

CONSOLIDATED STATEMENT OF CONDITION OF STATE SAVINGS AND LOAN ASSOCIATIONS IN TEXAS, DECEMBER 31, 1915

Assets

Loans on real estate	$1,088,029.01
Loans on stock	66,346.05
Interest accrued and unpaid	8,315.89
Fines, fees, etc.	1,729.81
Instalments on stock due and unpaid	35,115.17
Real estate	967.62
Sold on contract	574.15
Cash on hand	37,092.46
Other assets	9,132.37
Total assets	$1,247,302.53

Liabilities

Instalments on stock	$ 956,121.10
Instalments paid in advance	33,167.07
Instalments due and unpaid	26,173.10
Interest	7,147.61
Contingent fund	7,668.64
Profits divided	22,463.51
Profits undivided	129,902.71
Other liabilities	64,658.79
Total liabilities	$1,247,302.53

Source: *Forty-first Annual Report of the Commissioner of Insurance and Banking, 1916.* Austin, 1917, pp. 21–22.

TABLE 10

TOTAL ASSETS OF STATE SAVINGS AND LOAN ASSOCIATIONS IN TEXAS, DECEMBER 31, 1916

Texas associations (27) assets	$1,855,210.52
Foreign association (1) assets	$3,307,488.14
(no consolidated statement published in 1916)	

Source: *Forty-second Annual Report of the Commissioner of Insurance and Banking, 1917.* Austin, 1918, p. 24.

TABLE 11

CONSOLIDATED STATEMENT OF CONDITION OF STATE SAVINGS AND LOAN ASSOCIATIONS IN TEXAS, DECEMBER 31, 1917

Texas associations (29)

Assets

Loans on real estate	$2,041,545.87
Loans on stock	91,905.13
Interest accrued and unpaid	20,828.74
Premiums and fines, accrued and unpaid	1,993.40
Instalments on stock due and unpaid	25,086.69
Real estate	1,938.85
Real estate sold on contract	646.70
Accounts and bills receivable	33,798.59
Taxes advanced	318.49
Furniture and fixtures	2,420.90
Due from banks	58,457.40
Cash in hands of secretary and treasurer	28,742.54
Other resources	28,623.25
Insurance premiums advanced	625.94
Total assets	$2,366,832.49

Liabilities

Regular instalments paid in on stock	$1,725,761.36
Instalments on stock paid in advance	58,371.68
Instalments on stock due and unpaid	12,737.50
Stock paid up in advance	21,680.00
Interest and premiums paid in advance	78.40
Balance due on incomplete loans	5,281.18
Matured stock	10,250.00
Bills payable	80,977.80
Due treasurer	36.69
Outstanding orders	221.92
Interest	24,904.22
Contingent fund	10,601.22
Profit divided	94,893.91
Profit undivided	102,824.70
Other liabilities	188,211.91
Total liabilities	$2,366,832.49
Foreign association (1) assets	$3,432,472.61

Source: Forty-third Annual Report of the Commissioner of Insurance and Banking, 1918. Austin, 1919, pp. 22–23.
Note: The domestic assets in the above balance sheet do not add up to the total shown; however, they are reproduced as found in the annual report.

TABLE 12

CONSOLIDATED STATEMENT OF CONDITION OF STATE SAVINGS AND
LOAN ASSOCIATIONS IN TEXAS, DECEMBER 31, 1918

Texas associations (25)

Assets

Loans on real estate	$2,133,441.23
Loans on stock pledged	95,823.21
Interest accrued and unpaid	18,892.19
Premiums and fines, accrued and unpaid	2,416.22
Instalments on stock due and unpaid	20,873.36
Real estate	4,581.47
Real estate sold on contract	840.35
Accounts and bills receivable	47,250.48
Taxes advanced	388.85
Insurance premiums advanced	456.68
Furniture and fixtures	2,029.90
Due from banks	75,823.06
Cash in hands of treasurer and secretary	22,447.44
Other resources	59,696.47
Total assets	$2,484,958.91

Liabilities

Regular instalments paid in on stock	$1,814,573.99
Instalments on stock paid in advance	88,502.34
Instalments on stock due and unpaid	13,106.36
Stock paid up in advance	47,980.00
Interest premiums in advance	442.14
Balance due on incomplete loans	5,379.08
Matured stock	2,134.81
Bills payable	108,946.29
Outstanding orders	90.00
Interest	30,353.25
Contingent fund	41,007.96
Profit divided	63,531.40
Profit undivided	160,992.94
Other liabilities	107,928.35
Total liabilities	$2,484,958.91
Foreign association (1) assets	$3,862,645.15

Source: Forty-fourth Annual Report of the Commissioner of Insurance and Banking, 1919. Austin, 1920, pp. 34–39.
Note: The domestic assets and liabilities in the above balance sheet do not add up to the totals shown; however, they are reproduced as found in the annual report.

TABLE 13

CONSOLIDATED STATEMENT OF CONDITION OF STATE SAVINGS AND
LOAN ASSOCIATIONS IN TEXAS, DECEMBER 31, 1919

Texas associations (31)
Assets

Loans on real estate	$2,826,629.00
Loans on stock	109,698.22
Interest accrued and unpaid	12,964.52
Premiums and fines, accrued and unpaid	1,975.70
Instalments on stock due and unpaid	16,438.09
Real estate owned	4,726.01
Real estate sold on contract	356.45
Accounts and bills receivable	103,200.58
Taxes advanced	164.35
Insurance premiums advanced	331.67
Furniture and fixtures	12,003.69
Due from banks	65,377.08
Cash in hands of secretary and treasurer	63,111.82
Liberty bonds owned	30,458.80
Other resources	4,455.39
Total assets	$3,251,891.35

Liabilities

Regular instalments paid in on stock	$2,152,877.97
Instalments on stock paid in advance	148,532.31
Instalments on stock due and unpaid	10,629.59
Stock paid up in advance	103,480.00
Unearned premiums	
Interest and premiums paid in advance	16,353.29
Balance due on incomplete loans	33,226.17
Matured stock	12,815.85
Bills payable	337,459.81
Due treasurer	100,224.47
Outstanding orders	712.47
Insurance premiums	16.40
Interest	10,702.18
Contingent fund	17,086.91
Profit divided	104,728.78
Profit undivided	195,322.23
Other liabilities	7,722.92
Total liabilities	$3,251,891.35
Foreign associations (3) assets	$13,887,685.68

Source: Forty-fifth Annual Report of the Commissioner of Insurance and Banking, 1920. Austin, 1921, p. 20. Note: The domestic assets in the above balance sheet do not add up to the total shown; however, they are reproduced as found in the annual report.

TABLE 14

CONSOLIDATED STATEMENT OF CONDITION OF STATE SAVINGS AND LOAN ASSOCIATIONS IN TEXAS, DECEMBER 31, 1920

Texas associations (40)
Assets

Loans on real estate	$4,064,992.16
Loans on stock	173,686.99
Interest accrued and unpaid	14,364.72
Premiums and fines, accrued and unpaid	2,692.49
Instalments on stock due and unpaid	21,892.82
Real estate owned	5,509.29
Real estate sold on contract	191.45
Accounts and bills receivable	15,570.20
Taxes advanced	129.24
Insurance premiums advanced	354.54
Furniture and fixtures	4,355.91
Due from banks	43,064.48
Cash in hands of secretary and treasurer	70,862.13
Liberty bonds owned	29,332.16
Other resources	17,057.73
Total assets	**$4,464,056.31**

Liabilities

Regular instalments paid in on stock	$2,975,536.21
Instalments on stock paid in advance	290,210.92
Instalments on stock due and unpaid	15,842.82
Stock paid up in advance	351,158.34
Unearned premiums	364.10
Interest and premiums paid in advance	7,090.50
Balance due on incomplete loans	14,098.32
Matured stock	1,484.81
Bills payable	264,500.43
Due treasurer	12.08
Outstanding orders	....
Insurance premiums	5.37
Interest	26,425.64
Contingent fund	18,614.57
Profit divided	124,252.48
Profit undivided	242,603.81
Other liabilities	131,855.91
Total liabilities	**$4,464,056.31**
Foreign associations (4) assets	**$17,313,098.49**

Source: Forty-sixth Annual Report of the Commissioner of Insurance and Banking, 1921. Austin, 1922, p. 57.

TABLE 15

CONSOLIDATED STATEMENT OF CONDITION OF STATE SAVINGS AND LOAN ASSOCIATIONS IN TEXAS, DECEMBER 31, 1921

Texas associations (59)

Assets

Loans on real estate	$6,422,016.12
Loans on stock	344,975.14
Interest accrued and unpaid	26,138.14
Premiums and fines, accrued and unpaid	10,510.84
Instalments on stock due and unpaid	51,730.09
Real estate owned	17,565.96
Real estate sold on contract	510.00
Accounts and bills receivable	12,680.85
Taxes advanced	57.24
Insurance premiums advanced	2,430.26
Furniture and fixtures	13,861.29
Due from banks	108,514.12
Cash in hands of secretary and treasurer	109,623.36
Liberty bonds owned	13,976.12
Other resources	28,405.86
Total assets	**$7,162,995.29**

Liabilities

Regular instalments paid in on stock	$4,371,250.43
Instalments on stock paid in advance	398,036.99
Instalments on stock due and unpaid	41,687.34
Stock paid up in advance	1,154,354.39
Unearned premiums	131.87
Interest and premiums paid in advance	4,288.51
Balance due on incomplete loans	102,689.27
Matured stock	16,884.08
Bills payable	418,996.10
Due treasurer	766.41
Outstanding orders	798.43
Interest	32,504.15
Contingent fund	34,228.84
Profit divided	278,708.00
Profit undivided	288,427.65
Other liabilities	19,242.83
Total liabilities	**$7,162,995.29**
Foreign associations (4) assets	**$19,698,791.85**

Source: Forty-seventh Annual Report of the Commissioner of Insurance and Banking, 1922. Austin, 1923, p. 73.
Note: The domestic assets in the above balance sheet do not add up to the total shown; however, they are reproduced as found in the annual report.

TABLE 16

CONSOLIDATED STATEMENT OF CONDITION OF STATE SAVINGS AND
LOAN ASSOCIATIONS IN TEXAS, DECEMBER 31, 1922

Texas associations (82)

Assets

Loans on real estate	$10,895,860.04
Loans on stock	480,569.96
Interest accrued and unpaid	41,846.65
Premiums and fines, accrued and unpaid	22,757.53
Instalments on stock due and unpaid	65,451.47
Real estate owned	21,720.96
Real estate sold on contract	1,023.50
Accounts and bills receivable	17,351.93
Taxes advanced	573.44
Insurance premiums advanced	754.43
Furniture and fixtures	17,303.52
Due from banks	248,874.09
Cash in hands of secretary and treasurer	170,797.35
Liberty bonds owned	976.12
Other resources	53,383.14
Total assets	$12,039,244.13

Liabilities

Regular instalments paid in on stock	$7,006,223.77
Instalments on stock paid in advance	577,253.87
Instalments on stock due and unpaid	52,190.99
Stock paid up in advance	2,538,656.71
Unearned premiums	622.51
Interest and premiums paid in advance	9,836.68
Balance due on incomplete loans	157,361.74
Matured stock	192,952.38
Bills payable	421,382.17
Due treasurer	2,021.07
Outstanding orders	69,826.10
Interest	64,597.51
Contingent fund	48,879.96
Profit divided	426,056.56
Profit undivided	458,244.76
Other liabilities	13,137.35
Total liabilities	$12,039,244.13
Foreign associations (4)	assets $36,369,368.70

Source: *Forty-eighth Annual Report of the Commissioner of Insurance, 1923.* Austin, 1924, pp. 282–291.

TABLE 17

CONSOLIDATED STATEMENT OF CONDITION OF STATE SAVINGS AND
LOAN ASSOCIATIONS IN TEXAS, DECEMBER 31, 1923

Texas associations (87)

Assets

Loans on real estate	$19,191,253.76
Loans on stock pledged	759,355.25
Cash in hands and in banks	716,122.23
All other resources	393,151.32
Total assets	$21,060,250.33

Liabilities

Regular instalments paid in on stock	$12,114,773.84
Instalments on stock paid in advance	337,504.32
Instalments on stock due and unpaid	94,214.76
Stock paid up in advance	4,696,174.39
Profits undivided	681,763.40
All other liabilities	3,151,320.62
Total liabilities	$21,060,250.33
Foreign associations (4) assets	**$31,780,580.86**

Source: *Forty-ninth Annual Report of the Commissioner of Insurance, 1924.* Austin, 1925, pp. 182–186.
Note: *The domestic assets and liabilities in the above balance sheet do not add up to the totals shown; however, they are reproduced as found in the annual report.*

TABLE 18

CONSOLIDATED STATEMENT OF CONDITION OF STATE SAVINGS AND
LOAN ASSOCIATIONS IN TEXAS, DECEMBER 31, 1924

Texas associations (102)

Assets

Loans on real estate	$31,216,545.37
Loans on stock pledged	1,090,132.90
Cash in hand and in banks	1,007,884.58
All other resources	683,452.52
Total assets	$33,998,015.37

Liabilities

Regular instalments paid in on stock	$17,818,438.83
Instalments on stock paid in advance	2,334,932.49
Instalments on stock due and unpaid	270,895.70
Stock paid up in advance	7,860,371.73
Profits undivided	963,001.46
All other liabilities	4,750,375.16
Total liabilities	$33,998,015.37
Foreign associations (4) assets	**$39,570,419.73**

Source: *Fiftieth Annual Report of the Commissioner of Insurance, 1925.* Austin, 1926, pp. 164–169.

TABLE 19

CONSOLIDATED STATEMENT OF CONDITION OF STATE SAVINGS AND
LOAN ASSOCIATIONS IN TEXAS, DECEMBER 31, 1925

Texas associations (119)
Assets

Loans on real estate	$48,983,163.94
Loans on stock pledged	1,456,548.62
Cash in hand and in banks	740,084.20
All other resources	785,235.91
Total assets	$51,965,032.67

Liabilities

Regular instalments paid in on stock	$25,471,083.66
Instalments on stock paid in advance	4,173,930.95
Instalments on stock due and unpaid	263,387.32
Stock paid up in advance	10,889,016.04
Profits undivided	1,309,345.90
All other liabilities	9,858,268.80
Total liabilities	$51,965,032.67
Foreign associations (4) assets	$44,437,248.16

Source: *Fifty-first Annual Report of the Commissioner of Insurance, 1926.* Austin, 1927, pp. 176–182.

TABLE 20

CONSOLIDATED STATEMENT OF CONDITION OF STATE SAVINGS AND
LOAN ASSOCIATIONS IN TEXAS, DECEMBER 31, 1926

Texas associations (129)
Assets

Loans on real estate	$67,350,947.82
Loans on stock pledged	20,040,507.05
Cash in hand and in banks	489,803.04
All other resources	1,873,378.99
Total assets	$71,754,636.90

Liabilities

Regular instalments paid in on stock	$35,587,967.02
Instalments on stock paid in advance	4,609,484.58
Instalments on stock due and unpaid	376,314.53
Stock paid up in advance	16,004,325.77
Profits undivided	1,784,473.94
All other liabilities	13,392,071.06
Total liabilities	$71,754,636.90
Foreign associations (4) assets	$50,759,465.00

Source: *Fifty-second Annual Report of the Commissioner of Insurance, 1927.* Austin, 1928, pp. 191–194.
Note: *The domestic assets in the above balance sheet do not add up to the total shown; however, they are reproduced as found in the annual report.*

TABLE 21

CONSOLIDATED STATEMENT OF CONDITION OF STATE SAVINGS AND
LOAN ASSOCIATIONS IN TEXAS, DECEMBER 31, 1927

Texas associations (162)

Assets

Loans on real estate	$84,992,074.84
Loans on stock pledged	2,367,709.43
Cash in hand and in banks	2,025,718.20
All other resources	3,268,774.50
Total assets	$92,654,276.97

Liabilities

Regular instalments paid up on stock	$45,971,822.19
Instalments on stock paid in advance	5,940,725.77
Instalments on stock due and unpaid	817,441.36
Stock paid up in advance	22,269,752.96
Profits undivided	2,139,595.00
All other liabilities	15,514,939.69
Total liabilities	$92,654,276.97
Foreign associations (5) assets	$61,288,891.27

Source: *Fifty-third Annual Report of the Board of Insurance Commissioners, 1928.* Austin, 1929, pp. 205–216.

TABLE 22

CONSOLIDATED STATEMENT OF CONDITION OF STATE SAVINGS AND
LOAN ASSOCIATIONS IN TEXAS, DECEMBER 31, 1929

Texas associations (176)

Assets

Real estate loans	$122,886,727.22
Stock loans	3,946,277.41
Bonds, securities, etc.	211,411.70
Due from banks	2,420,325.36
Cash	242,077.19
Interest earned, not collected	866,299.61
Insurance, taxes, etc., paid for members	111,869.81
Accounts due from officers and employees	10,921.66
Accounts receivable	109,884.24
Real estate acquired by foreclosure	3,235,282.07
Furniture and fixtures	302,776.13
Other assets	2,672,051.31
Total assets	$137,015,903.71

(Continued on next page.)

TABLE 22 (Continued)

Liabilities

Withdrawable shares	$118,802,741.17
Reserve or permanent stock	1,803,820.79
Legal reserve	680,663.85
Undivided profits	1,557,449.89
Other reserves	482,207.72
Dividends accrued	2,246,581.40
Interest paid but not accrued	26,303.83
Incomplete loans	516,632.19
Borrowed money	3,117,535.13
Accounts payable	84,927.28
Other liabilities	1,697,040.46
Total liabilities	$137,015,903.71
Foreign associations (6)	assets $89,305,874.49

Source: First Annual Report of Building and Loan Associations, 1929, p. 4.
Note: The domestic liabilities in the above balance sheet do not add up to the total shown; however, they are reproduced as found in the annual report.

The Period 1930–1936

The year 1929 marks a natural breaking point in savings and loan history. State legislation enacted in that year changed the legal rules under which savings and loan associations operated, and the depression which followed caused drastic changes in nearly all phases of savings and loan activity.

The period extending from 1930 through 1936, though only seven years in duration, was one of great changes. While the years immediately preceding 1929 were characterized by optimism and growth, those from 1930 to 1936 can be described as years of pessimism and contraction. By 1936 the immediate adjustments to the depression had been made, the savings and loan industry was beginning to see a glimmer of recovery, and the federal institutions that were to influence so greatly savings and loan activities had crystallized into fairly permanent form. Of course many subsequent acts by the federal government were to affect savings and loan activity, but the institutions dealing exclusively and primarily with savings and loan associations had been organized by that time. Also, 1936 saw the re-election of the Democratic administration which indicated that federal activity would continue— for another four years at least—along the lines already established.

The period 1930 to 1936 began with a total of 176 state associations and ended with 95 active state associations and 14 in liquidation. At the beginning of the period, total assets of the associations amounted to over $137 million; at the end, assets of active state associations were valued at less than $60 million. Part of this decrease can be explained by conversion from state into federal associations, for such conversion was quite common during this period.

Table 23 presents the changes in number of state associations and their resources from 1929 through 1936. For ease in comparison with the prior period, the figures for the year 1929 are included in this and other tables in this chapter.

TABLE 23

TEXAS SAVINGS AND LOAN ASSOCIATIONS, 1929 TO 1936

Year	Number of associations	Total assets
1929	176 state	$137,015,903
1930	155 state	134,743,150
1931	145 state	127,285,977
1932	144 state	114,631,152
1933	139 active state	100,393,588
	4 liquidating state	742,712
	143 total	101,136,300
1934	130 active state	82,886,876
	3 liquidating state	479,561
	54 federal	3,556,150
	187 total	86,922,587
1935	98 active state	61,742,963
	14 liquidating state	1,960,873
	86 federal	14,366,932
	198 total	70,070,768
1936	95 active state	59,246,444
	14 liquidating state	1,716,330
	88 federal	18,468,693
	197 total	79,427,467

Source: Annual Report of Building and Loan Associations, 1929–1936; Building and Loan Annals, 1930–1937.

Table 23 shows that during the seven years from the beginning of 1930 through 1936, total assets of all active state associations declined by over $77,000,000, nearly 57 percent. When the total assets of all associations operating in 1936, including both federal and liquidating state associations are considered, the decline amounts to $61,000,000, or over 44 percent. The 95 active state associations, the 14 liquidating, and the 88 federal associations held assets valued at only slightly over 55 percent of the amount held by the 176 associations at the opening of the period. In 1930, the average size of each association, measured by assets, was $778,503. In 1936 the average for the active state associations was $630,281; for the liquidating state associations, $122,595; and for the federal associations, $168,724. From this, as well as from other information contained in the annual reports of the Banking Commission, it may correctly be assumed that the greatest number of liquidations and conversions to federal associations occurred among the smaller associations. While there may be little to recommend size as such, it does tend to impart stability to an association.

During the 1930–36 period, fifteen associations consolidated with other state associations. These consolidations occurred during 1930 and 1931. There were no additional consolidations from 1932 to 1936. Consolidation was an early attempt to prevent failure and seems to have been successful in most instances. By 1936 all but one of the associations which consolidated were still in existence. However, one of the consolidated associations reorganized in 1933 with a change in name, and another converted to a federal association in 1935.

Texas savings and loan legislation in effect from 1930 through 1936 provided that the affairs of an association could be terminated in one of two ways: (a) by being placed in receivership, or (b) by going into voluntary liquidation. Under certain conditions[14] the banking commissioner was empowered to initiate action to revoke a charter and to have a receiver appointed to conclude the affairs of an association. Writing in the 1931 annual report James Shaw, the Banking Commissioner, stated:

When associations are placed in receivership this department has nothing further to do with them. The receivers are appointed by the Court, and are handled the same as receiverships in any other corporation.[15]

In addition, stockholders of associations were permitted to vote to go into voluntary liquidation and to allow the association to handle the termination itself; the court did not appoint a receiver. Mr. Shaw comments on this by saying:

An amendment to the law had been passed which places associations in voluntary liquidation under the supervision of the Banking Commissioner, and further provides that all sales of assets and all expenses shall be approved by the Banking Commissioner before such sales are made or expenses incurred.[16]

Between 1930 and 1936 a total of forty-nine associations took steps which led to their termination: ten were placed in receivership, twenty-three either completed voluntary liquidation or were sold, and sixteen others began the process of voluntary liquidation and subsequently completed liquidation.

Savings and loan legislation also provided that stockholders could vote, under certain conditions, to reorganize their associations under their existing charters. Later provisions were made to allow reorganization under a new charter and, if desired, under a new name. J. A. Pratt, Building and Loan

[14] See Chapter IV.
[15] *Third Annual Report of Building and Loan Associations, 1931* (n.p.), p. 6.
[16] *Ibid.*

Supervisor, describes the reorganization privilege in the *Sixth Annual Report of Building and Loan Associations* (1933) in the following words:

> Section 21a relating to reorganizations has been changed so as to provide for reorganizations, in whole or in part, under either the State or Federal laws, and for the creation of another association for the purpose of transferring a part of the assets, properties, engagements and funds of the association being reorganized. . . . [17]

Because of the provision that a new association could be created to hold the more liquid assets and the old association used as a liquidating device, the statistics provided in the annual reports of the banking commissioners may present a misleading picture of the extent of savings and loan formation during this period. What appears to be the organization of several new associations becomes, upon closer scrutiny, merely the legal action necessary to effect a reorganization under Section 21a. (See Chapter IV.) For this reason, Tables 24 and 25 divide the associations which have reorganized into those which reorganized by writing down their assets and retaining their old charters and those which, in effect, reorganized because they transferred part of their assets to newly chartered associations and liquidated the old associations.

Five associations reorganized under the same name and retained their original charters during this period. These associations are listed in Table 24. In addition to these five, one other association, the Colonial Building and Loan Association of San Angelo, which had previously gone through a consolidation, reorganized under a new name: the Capital Building and Loan Association.

TABLE 24

TEXAS SAVINGS AND LOAN ASSOCIATIONS REORGANIZED
UNDER SAME CHARTER

Name	Location	Date
North American	Dallas	1934
Citizens	Fort Worth	1933
San Antonio	San Antonio	1932*
Security	San Antonio	1932
Citizens	Fort Worth	1933
North Texas	Wichita Falls	1933
North American	Dallas	1934

Source: Annual Report of Building and Loan Associations, 1932–1934.
* The reorganization of the San Antonio Savings and Loan Association was accomplished without a loss to the owners of repurchasable shares.

[17] *Sixth Annual Report of Building and Loan Associations, 1933,* Foreword.

Between 1930 and 1936, eight associations obtained new charters and segregated their assets, transferring the better assets to the new association. These are, for all practical purposes, reorganizations and are presented in Table 25.

TABLE 25

TEXAS SAVINGS AND LOAN ASSOCIATIONS REORGANIZED
UNDER DIFFERENT CHARTER

Name	Location	New name and date of organization
Beaumont Building and Loan Company	Beaumont	Beaumont Building and Loan Association, 1934
Texas Plains	Amarillo	Great Plains Building and Loan, 1934
Bell County	Belton	Bell County Federal Savings and Loan, 1935
Home Building and Loan Company	Beaumont	Home Building and Loan Association, 1935
Security	San Antonio	First Federal Savings and Loan Association, 1935
Tarrant County	Fort Worth	Tarrant County of Fort Worth Building and Loan, 1935
Abilene	Abilene	Anchor Building and Loan, 1936
Plainview	Plainview	Home Building and Loan, 1936

Source: Annual Report of Building and Loan Associations, 1934–1936.

Of the eight reorganizations, two were under federal charters. In addition, the Metropolitan Building and Loan Association of Dallas was organized in 1932 with the same directors and officers as the Continental Southland Savings and Loan Association. The Continental Southland began liquidation after 1936. As a consequence, the Metropolitan may be considered a reorganization rather than a "new" association.

After the new associations that were organized to hold part of the assets of existing associations are removed from the list of new charters issued by the Department of Banking during this period, only two remain: the Southern Building and Loan Association of Athens and the Mutual Building and Loan Association of Fort Worth. The Southern was dissolved the same year in which it was organized, 1935. So, in effect, only one new association was organized during the period, 1930 through 1936.

The primary problem faced by savings and loan associations from 1930 through 1936 was one of survival. With the great decline in mortgages outstanding, as seen in Table 26, income declined greatly. Serious as this was, the increase in foreclosures during this period was even more damaging.

Table 27 presents statistics on real estate owned by associations and shows that a high of $17,966,673 was reached in 1935.

The high foreclosures can be explained by many factors; of course the general decline in real estate values during the period was the main cause, but in addition many practices during prior periods which permitted high-percentage financing and unsound policies contributed to the seriousness of the situation.

TABLE 26

MORTGAGE LOANS OF TEXAS SAVINGS AND LOAN ASSOCIATIONS,
1929 TO 1936

Year	Mortgage loans outstanding	Percent of assets
1929	$122,886,727	89.6
1930	119,681,266	88.9
1931	110,740,498	87.0
1932	90,410,170	78.8
1933	76,960,311	76.0
1934		
State	51,595,499	59.1
Federal	2,187,899	72.1
Total	53,783,398	61.8
1935		
State	36,513,361	62.3
Federal	10,359,680	61.5
Total	46,873,041	62.0
1936		
State	37,470,070	63.2
Federal	15,146,724	82.0
Total	52,616,794	66.2

Source: Building and Loan Annals, 1930–1937.

TABLE 27

FORECLOSED REAL ESTATE OF TEXAS SAVINGS AND LOAN ASSOCIATIONS,
1929 TO 1936

Year	Number of properties	Value of properties	Percent of total assets
1929	n.a.	$ 3,235,282	2.36
1930	1,541	4,018,190	2.98
1931	3,148	6,791,318	5.33
1932	6,537	13,132,631	11.45
1933	8,206	16,321,194	16.13
1934	n.a.	15,888,410	18.27
1935	n.a.	17,966,673	24.73
1936	n.a.	16,058,093	20.00

Source: Savings and Loan Annals, 1930–1937.

Largely because the era preceding the period between 1930 and 1936 was one of growth and optimism, savings and loan associations had concentrated upon building volume and paid little attention to reserves and other factors which might have placed them in a better position when it came to meeting the withdrawal demands of depositors and absorbing the losses sustained upon foreclosed real estate. One manifestation of this lack of interest in reserves and like devices is to be found in the *Savings and Loan Annals*. In the 1931 issue, one writer states, while discussing secondary reserves:

I talked to a man who is in charge of the building and loan associations in the State of Illinois. He said he knew of only one association in his district which had any kind of a reserve of this kind, but said they got into difficulty because they invested it in mortgages, the very thing they should not have done because the large percentage of their assets consisted of that type of investment.[18]

In the 1936 annals many articles are devoted to a determination of correct reserves, useful ratios, and other tests of liquidity and safety to be employed by a firm. If the depression did nothing else, it brought to the front the use of reserves. In an effort to meet these problems, the associations of the state could and did attempt many remedies. For some associations the case was, or appeared to be, hopeless. They were liquidated, either voluntarily or involuntarily. Others tried to cope with the situation by consolidations. This, as mentioned earlier, had some success. Others suffered their loss and reorganized. Still others tried to escape the dilemma by converting to federal associations. Of the eighty-eight federal associations operating in the state on December 31, 1936, twenty-nine were converted state associations.

The year 1936 was the last prewar year in which there were more state than federal associations in Texas. There are many reasons for this conversion to federal associations. Doubtless some associations converted for the added prestige that might go with a federal charter; others desired to obtain share insurance. The Federal Savings and Loan Insurance Corporation made provisions, it is true, for insurance of shares in both state and federal associations. However, while insurance of shares was automatic with federal associations, state associations were subjected to a long and severe test before being accepted. This was a period when all associations were faced with great withdrawal demands. Share insurance did much to allay suspicions and stop withdrawals. Many state associations doubted that they could meet withdrawals while waiting to be approved for share insurance and so converted to federal charters.

Mr. Bristow, the Commissioner of Insurance and Banking of Virginia, had this to say on the subject of insurance of shares in state associations:

[18] George P. Ellis, "The Monthly Comparative Balance Sheet," *Building and Loan Annals, 1931* (Chicago: The United States Building and Loan League), p. 246.

I think it will be conceded that the Federal Savings and Loan Insurance System was designed to offer to building and loan associations virtually the same protection as has been given to banks. The experience which we have just had in regard to the admission of banks into their system should be illuminating to us for the admission of building and loan associations into their system. I have been basing my hopes accordingly. It would be my disposition to urge all building and loan associations to apply for insurance if the standards and tests would be approximately the same as for banks. I freely admit that the same test applied to banks cannot properly be used for building and loan associations. Still, the objective should be practically the same and, therefore, the phrasing or wording of the standard set should be changed accordingly. I cannot speak for other supervisors but, I believe, if similar tests to those applied to the banks of my state were applied to the building and loan associations in it, a large majority of the latter would be accepted.[19]

Most would admit that the Federal Savings and Loan Insurance Corporation did not give equal treatment to both federal and state associations—an unfortunate situation.

It has already been pointed out that during 1930 through 1936 the State of Texas chartered only one truly new savings and loan association. During the same period eighty-eight federal associations were chartered in the state. Of these, twenty-nine were the conversions referred to above; the other fifty-nine were new associations. In order to encourage the organization of new associations and the conversion of existing ones, the federal government actively pushed federal savings and loan associations, as a device to place more mortgage money and hence encourage recovery.[20] This may have been justified in some instances, but of the fifty-nine new federal associations organized, twenty-three were organized in cities which already had at least one state association. Today, the state seems to have advanced to a stage at which it can accommodate the great number of associations it contains; but the wisdom of creating a competitive type of association rather than strengthening the ones already in existence is questionable.

One other example of the pressure to convert to a federal charter is contained in a speech by John F. Scott of Saint Paul, Minnesota. In discussing the growth of his association since converting to a federal charter, he says of the assistance derived from the Home Owners Loan Corporation:

[19] M. E. Bristow, "Federalization of Building and Loan Associations," *Building and Loan Annals, 1934* (Chicago: The United States Building and Loan League), p. 333.

[20] Representatives from the Federal Home Loan Bank of Little Rock made trips through Texas meeting with local groups in an effort to encourage and assist them in the formation of federal associations. In most instances, the initiative was taken by the representative of the Home Loan Bank; in one case the writer knows of, the group contacted did not know what a savings and loan association was. Ususally, HOLC would agree to make a sizable investment in the proposed newly-created or converted federal association.

We have done this by the use today of $3,000,000 of Home Owner's Loan Corporation investment in our fully paid income shares. $3,000,000: . . .

I have no better shareholder than that Home Owners' Loan Corporation. The Corporation has guaranteed that it will not repurchase for five years, and thereafter will not ask for the repurchase of more than 10 per cent of its investment in any one year. It is my biggest shareholder. It has 50 votes in my institution. The Corporation has invested $3,000,000 and I am going to have it invest several million more until the rest of you folks get together with your applications for HOLC money and stimulate a loan demand in your community. . . .[21]

The Home Owners Loan Corporation, while it would place funds with insured state associations, seemed to show preferential treatment to federal associations.

By 1936, the savings and loan industry in Texas found itself in a position by no means secure; but it had greatly improved and strengthened its position over what it had been a few years earlier. While the industry, mainly because of the impact of federal government activities, was to emerge from this period in a form greatly altered from that with which the period was begun, the situation appeared to be improving, and most believed that better times were to come.

The following pages contain consolidated balance sheets of Texas savings and loan associations from 1930 through 1936.

[21] John F. Scott, "Building Loan Volume With HOLC Funds," *Building and Loan Annals,* 1936 (Chicago: The United States Building and Loan League), p. 297.

TABLE 28

CONSOLIDATED STATEMENT OF CONDITION OF STATE SAVINGS AND
LOAN ASSOCIATIONS IN TEXAS, DECEMBER 31, 1930

Texas associations (155)
Assets

Real estate	$119,681,266.13
Stock loans	4,466,411.09
Bonds, securities, etc.	69,735.66
Due from banks	2,492,608.01
Cash	280,673.91
Interest earned, not collected	1,108,718.87
Insurance, taxes, etc. paid for members	129,016.73
Accounts due from officers and employees	2,526.58
Accounts receivable	62,060.07
Real estate acquired by foreclosure	4,018,190.43
Furniture and fixtures	286,563.58
Other assets	2,145,379.52
Total assets	$134,743,150.58

Liabilities

Withdrawable shares	$123,228,129.29
Reserve fund or permanent stock	1,538,292.90
Legal reserve	763,136.35
Undivided profits	1,399,518.81
Other reserves	604,105.63
Dividends accrued	2,372,063.51
Interest paid but not accrued	25,213.38
Incomplete loans	348,165.05
Borrowed money	2,794,795.54
Accounts payable	54,008.66
Other liabilities	1,615,721.46
Total liabilities	$134,743,150.58
Foreign associations (5)	assets $90,760,323.93

Source: Second Annual Report of Building and Loan Associations, 1930, p. 9.

TABLE 29

CONSOLIDATED STATEMENT OF CONDITION OF STATE SAVINGS AND
LOAN ASSOCIATIONS IN TEXAS, DECEMBER 31, 1931

Texas associations (145)

Assets

Real estate loans	$110,740,498.55
Stock loans	3,460,282.42
Bonds, securities, etc.	123,404.51
Due from banks	1,804,451.23
Cash	114,172.44
Interest earned, not collected	1,329,395.18
Insurance, taxes, etc. paid for members	147,189.66
Accounts due from officers and employees	3,085.84
Accounts receivable	38,352.86
Real estate acquired by foreclosure	6,791,318.54
Furniture and fixtures	295,560.68
Other assets	2,438,266.07
Total assets	$127,285,977.98

Liabilities

Withdrawable stock	$117,207,931.65
Reserve fund or permanent stock	1,965,656.15
Legal reserve	701,411.43
Undivided profits	1,606,504.84
Other reserves	1,023,094.97
Dividends accrued	1,455,456.38
Interest paid but not accrued	17,023.24
Incomplete loans	35,538.82
Borrowed money	2,778,035.43
Accounts payable	89,925.04
Other liabilities	405,400.03
Total liabilities	$127,285,977.98
Foreign associations (4) assets	$ 80,577,346.09

Source: Third Annual Report of Building and Loan Associations, 1931, p. 9.

TABLE 30

CONSOLIDATED STATEMENT OF CONDITION OF STATE SAVINGS AND LOAN ASSOCIATIONS IN TEXAS, DECEMBER 31, 1932

Texas associations (144)

Assets

Real estate loans	$90,410,170.13
Stock loans	2,169,143.20
Bonds, securities	73,567.27
Due from banks	1,556,045.39
Cash	105,933.85
Interest earned, not collected	1,364,528.44
Insurance, taxes, etc. paid for members	364,566.00
Accounts due from officers and employees	3,388.04
Accounts receivable	68,399.92
Real estate acquired by foreclosure	13,132,631.13
Furniture and fixtures	250,917.07
Other assets	5,131,862.29
Total assets	$114,631,152.73

Liabilities

Withdrawable shares	$100,066,344.73
Reserve fund or permanent stock	1,816,319.99
Legal reserve	1,092,737.77
Undivided profits	1,036,773.89
Other reserves	3,571,763.21
Dividends accrued	1,241,696.29
Interest paid but not accrued	52,318.58
Incomplete loans	42,171.79
Borrowed money	3,331,301.58
Accounts payable	191,292.72
Other liabilities	2,188,432.18
Total liabilities	$114,631,152.73
Foreign associations (3) assets	$ 27,030,353.93

Source: Fourth Annual Report of Building and Loan Associations, 1932, p. 7.

TABLE 31

CONSOLIDATED STATEMENT OF CONDITION OF STATE SAVINGS AND
LOAN ASSOCIATIONS IN TEXAS, DECEMBER 31, 1933

Texas associations (139)
Assets

Real estate loans	$75,903,043.28
Real estate sold on contract	1,057,267.40
Stock loans	1,603,341.73
Stock in Federal Home Loan Bank	398,325.00
Bonds, securities, etc.	639,315.99
Cash due from banks and on hand	1,469,994.03
Interest earned, not collected	1,531,720.42
Insurance, taxes, etc. paid for members	430,971.23
Accounts receivable	118,827.03
Real estate acquired	16,321,193.89
Real estate—home office building	329,239.91
Furniture and fixtures	186,963.13
Other assets	376,385.54
Total assets	$100,393,588.58

Liabilities

Withdrawable shares	$ 84,311,864.13
Reserve fund or permanent stock	1,537,704.46
Legal reserve	1,465,883.83
Undivided profits	1,718,727.21
Other reserves	4,322,096.92
Dividends accrued	786,013.52
Interest paid but not accrued	10,514.91
Incomplete loans	92,273.18
Borrowed money	3,663,880.48
Accounts payable	145,736.28
Other liabilities	2,338,893.66
Total liabilities	$100,393,588.58
Foreign associations (4) assets	$ 53,583,155.18

Source: *Fifth Annual Report of Building and Loan Associations, 1933, p. 9.*
Note: *The domestic assets in the above balance sheet do not add up to the total shown; however, they are reproduced as found in the annual report.*

TABLE 32

CONSOLIDATED STATEMENT OF CONDITION OF STATE SAVINGS AND
LOAN ASSOCIATIONS IN TEXAS, DECEMBER 31, 1934

Texas associations (130)

Assets

Real estate loans	$51,595,499.06
Real estate sold on contract	831,738.63
Stock loans	1,617,364.09
Stock in Federal Home Loan Bank	461,723.19
Bonds, securities, etc.	7,578,411.27
Cash due from banks and on hand	1,939,399.70
Interest earned, not collected	1,240,312.29
Insurance, taxes, paid for members	372,515.73
Accounts receivable	78,484.50
Real estate acquired	15,278,373.75
Real estate—home office building	432,627.08
Furniture and fixtures	168,432.37
Other assets	1,291,994.84
Total assets	$82,886,876.50

Liabilities

Withdrawable shares	$69,517,459.83
Reserve or permanent fund	1,538,995.69
Legal reserve	1,315,197.56
Undivided profits	1,492,728.63
Other reserves	5,125,501.69
Dividends accrued	629,603.50
Interest paid but not accrued	11,384.18
Incomplete loans	63,309.96
Borrowed money	3,044,699.44
Accounts payable	81,025.64
Other liabilities	66,970.38
Total liabilities	$82,886,876.50
Foreign associations (3) assets	$39,903,661.69
Federal associations (54) assets	$ 3,556,150.00

Source: Sixth Annual Report of Building and Loan Associations, 1934, p. 3.

TABLE 33

CONSOLIDATED STATEMENT OF CONDITION OF STATE SAVINGS AND
LOAN ASSOCIATIONS IN TEXAS, DECEMBER 31, 1935

Texas associations (98)
Assets

Real estate loans	$35,734,300.80
Real estate owned and sold on contract	17,418,789.81
Stock loans	1,184,980.07
Federal Home Loan Bank stock	377,831.22
Bonds, securities, etc.	2,612,823.87
Other interest bearing assets	741,912.59
Cash due from banks and on hand	2,125,327.32
Interest earned but not collected	434,644.14
Insurance, taxes, etc. paid for members	159,191.67
Accounts receivable	104,405.81
Furniture and fixtures	140,788.04
Home office building	491,899.25
Other assets	216,068.55
Total assets	$61,742,963.14

Liabilities

Withdrawable stock	$48,919,366.05
Permanent stock	1,330,633.34
Other stock	1,087,518.89
Legal reserve	1,118,010.36
Undivided profits	1,103,006.95
Other reserves	3,968,245.46
Dividends accrued	487,552.67
Interest accrued	8,697.35
Incomplete loans	282,314.51
Borrowed money	1,864,844.67
Accounts payable	742,805.65
Other liabilities	121,534.49
Federal Home Loan Bank advances	612,679.09
Federal insurance	95,753.66
Total liabilities	$61,742,963.14
Foreign associations (3) assets	$35,641,066.95
Federal associations (86) assets	$14,366,932.00

Source: Seventh Annual Report of Building and Loan Associations, 1935, p. 3.

TABLE 34

CONSOLIDATED STATEMENT OF CONDITION OF STATE SAVINGS AND
LOAN ASSOCIATIONS IN TEXAS, DECEMBER 31, 1936

Texas associations (95)
Assets

First mortgage and other loans	$38,635,865.01
Real estate owned and sold on contract	15,437,517.75
Stock in Federal Home Loan Banks	359,125.00
U. S. government bonds and other securities	1,444,509.36
Cash on hand and in banks	1,996,338.34
Office buildings (net)	449,492.85
Furniture and fixtures (net)	75,348.46
Other assets	848,636.43
Total assets	$59,246,883.20

Liabilities

Free or repurchasable shares	$43,667,115.22
Mortgage pledged shares	4,343,201.12
Advances and borrowed money	2,829,631.58
Advance payments by borrowers for taxes and insurance	84,031.90
Dividends declared and unpaid	315,335.72
Other liabilities	1,097,513.24
Permanent reserve or guaranty stock	1,236,000.00
Reserves and undivided profits	5,674,054.42
Total liabilities	$59,246,883.20
Foreign associations (3) assets	$34,287,790.32
Federal associations (88) assets	$18,468,693.00

Source: *Eighth Annual Report of Building and Loan Associations, 1936*, pp. 2–3.

CHAPTER VI

Savings and Loan Associations in Texas, 1937–1953

From 1937 through 1953, there were great changes in the savings and loan industry in Texas. For purposes of analyzing these changes, the era from 1937 through 1953 will be divided into two periods. The first, 1937–1945, begins with the year in which the savings and loan industry in Texas was emerging from the depression and ends with the close of World War II. The second period, 1946–1953, traces the changes in the savings and loan industry during the greatest building boom the state of Texas has ever witnessed.

The Period 1937–1945

On December 31, 1937, there were 176 active associations in the state—87 domestic and 89 federal. On the same date in 1945 there were 139 associations—52 state and 87 federal. (See Table 35.) Although this is a decline in the number of associations, during this same period the assets of savings and loan associations in Texas increased from $83,716,153 to $160,733,000. Probably more important than the increase in total assets was the improvement in the quality of the assets.

Table 36 shows that during this period total assets of savings and loan associations in Texas enjoyed a steady, though not spectacular, growth; in no single year did assets increase as much as 15 percent. But during this period

TABLE 35

NUMBER OF SAVINGS AND LOAN ASSOCIATIONS IN TEXAS, 1937 TO 1945

Year	State	Federal	Total
1937	87	89	176
1938	71	90	161
1939	62	91	153
1940	58	91	149
1941	63	92	155
1942	52	92	144
1943	50	92	142
1944	51	90	141
1945	52	87	139

Source: *Savings and Loan Annals, 1938–1946.* Annual Report.

any increase at all was cause for thankfulness. In twelve states, assets decreased in 1937. In Pennsylvania the decrease alone amounted to more than the total assets of all savings and loan associations in Texas, and as late as 1943 assets in two states decreased. In one year—1938 only—assets of state-chartered associations in Texas decreased. Even though the number of state associations decreased steadily until 1944, their total assets, with the exception noted above, increased. The decrease in 1938 can be explained by unusually heavy liquidations—12 associations were liquidated and dissolved; two were converted into federals.

The general increase in assets during these nine years can be explained

TABLE 36

TOTAL ASSETS OF SAVINGS AND LOAN ASSOCIATIONS IN TEXAS,
1937 TO 1945

Year	State	Federal	Total	Increase over previous year
1937	$59,530,001	$24,186,152	$ 83,716,153	$ 6,001,015
1938	46,466,945	44,895,492	91,362,437	7,646,284
1939	47,976,272	47,217,804	95,194,076	3,831,639
1940	48,693,818	53,813,472	102,507,290	7,313,214
1941	49,369,461	68,186,000	117,555,461	15,048,171
1942	50,490,696	68,993,083	119,483,779	1,928,318
1943	54,013,310	71,515,709	125,529,019	6,045,240
1944	62,598,264	76,753,955	139,352,219	13,813,200
1945	75,447,000	85,286,000	160,733,000	21,380,781

Source: Savings and Loan Annals, 1938–1946.

by two factors: the increased level of income in Texas and returned confidence in savings and loan associations. In the years from 1937 through 1945, Texas enjoyed a high degree of industrialization, which resulted in greatly increased incomes. Consumer goods were in short supply during the war years, and savings quite naturally increased. The fact that increased savings came to be invested in savings and loan associations can be explained by the growing confidence investors placed in the industry.

Savings and loan associations, like other financial institutions, suffered a serious loss of reputation during the depression. As a result of failures, many investors lost savings, which, quite naturally, left them with a reluctance to reinvest in such institutions. Before the industry could hope to grow, distrust had to be dispelled. During the 1930's, a good deal of effort was expended by savings and loan associations, both individually and collectively through leagues and other groups, to restore confidence in the industry. An examination of the *Building and Loan Annals* for those years will disclose that a seemingly disproportionate part of the time of the annual convention was devoted to advertising and other activities designed to improve the public relations of associations. One manifestation of this atttude is to be found in the talk of E. L. Wells, Jr., of Marshall, Texas, delivered at the 1938 annual convention of the United States Building and Loan League. Mr. Wells states:

The general American public's estimate of building and loan needs to be worked over. One very important and indispensable phase of this job must, in my opinion, be accomplished through national advertising. We have to deal with a national condition and it must be handled in a national way.[1]

Advertising, coupled with improving conditions within savings and loan associations, doubtless did much to allay the suspicions which had developed.

In all probability, increased advertising did stimulate investments in savings and loan associations, but even more important were the activities of the federal government. The Federal Savings and Loan Insurance Corporation provided for share insurance, thereby increasing the safety of such investments. It is true that initially this insurance did not provide for immediate payment, but the safety which it was believed to impart to such investments tended to restore confidence. The Home Loan Banks have, through the use of advances, successfully given liquidity to the assets of member associations; doubtless, the mere existence of the Home Loan Banks, with their implied promise to come to the aid of members, helped restore confidence in the industry. Also, insurance of loans by the Federal Housing Authority removed a large part of the risk from a portion of the investments of the associations. The various institutions created by the federal government will be discussed in a later chapter, but there were many of them, and they all helped build faith in savings and loan associations in Texas. Some would say that the chief contribution of the federal government to the savings and loan field was the restoring of confidence in the industry.

Between 1937 and 1945 the quality of assets owned by savings and loan associations changed greatly. In 1937 savings and loan associations owned over $10 million worth of real estate other than office buildings. By 1945 this figure had been reduced to slightly over $1 million. The ratio of real estate owned, exclusive of office buildings, to total assets declined from over 12 percent to less than 0.1 percent. This resulted from the improved market for real estate which made it possible for associations to dispose of holdings which had been acquired through foreclosure. Table 37 presents these changes from 1937 through 1945.

Table 38 lists the amount of lending completed each year from 1937 through 1945. Compared with later years the amount is small, but there was

[1] Wells, E. L. Jr., "Discussion Period," *Building and Loan Annals, 1938* (Chicago: United States Building and Loan League, 1938), p. 322.

TABLE 37

REAL ESTATE (NOT INCLUDING OFFICE BUILDINGS) OWNED BY TEXAS
SAVINGS AND LOAN ASSOCIATIONS, 1937 TO 1945

Year	State	Federal	Total
1937	$9,487,354	$775,922	$10,263,276
1938	7,005,390	873,920	7,879,310
1939	2,188,218	709,282	2,897,500
1940	3,480,746	593,906	4,074,652
1941	1,849,131	504,000	2,353,131
1942	693,090	262,413	955,503
1943	375,868	104,241	480,109
1944	247,000	76,000	323,000
1945	54,000	58,000	112,000

Source: Savings and Loan Annals, 1938–1946.

TABLE 38

MORTGAGE LOANS MADE BY TEXAS SAVINGS AND LOAN
ASSOCIATIONS, 1937 TO 1945

Year	State	Federal	Total
1937	$11,788,013	$ 8,533,295	$20,321,308
1938	11,352,766	10,987,983	22,340,749
1939	13,251,549	13,754,412	27,005,961
1940	21,637,872	13,585,856	35,223,728
1941	13,784,313	17,499,000	31,283,313
1942	n.a.	10,794,800	n.a.
1943	14,645,824	16,123,500	30,769,324
1944	668,000	21,231,000	21,899,000
1945	22,209,000	27,085,000	49,294,000

Source: Savings and Loan Annals, 1938–1946.

little real estate activity and less new private construction during this period. The amount of mortgage loans outstanding declined during 1942 and 1943, and the percentage of mortgage loans to total assets reached a low of 71 percent in 1945. (See Table 39.) The shortage of mortgage outlets gave rise to another type of investment: government bonds. While the bonds were low-yield assets and were not preferred by most associations, they did improve the liquidity of the associations and imparted a degree of stability.

From 1937 to 1945 the surplus and undivided profits accounts of savings and loan associations in Texas increased substantially. On December 31, 1937, surplus and undivided profits amounted to $6,961,126; on the same date in 1945, these accounts amounted to $13,694,000, as shown by Table 40.

There was a sharp decline in the surplus accounts of state associations in 1938, caused by the unusually heavy liquidation and conversion rate, but the total decline in these accounts for all associations amounted to little more than $500,000. Inasmuch as surplus and undivided profits tend to strengthen associations, the industry emerged from this period much stronger than it entered it.

The increased reserves of savings and loan associations can be accounted for in part by requirements of regulatory agencies. The State Banking Commission, the Home Loan Bank System, and The Federal Savings and Loan Insurance Corporation all require that the institutions they supervise provide

TABLE 39

MORTGAGE INVESTMENTS OF TEXAS SAVINGS AND LOAN
ASSOCIATIONS, 1937 TO 1945

Year	State	Federal	Total	Increase over previous year	Percent total mtge. loans to assets
1937	$42,139,057	$20,941,609	$ 63,080,666	$10,463,872	75.4
1938	38,453,315	33,873,435	72,326,750	9,246,084	79.1
1939	32,818,109	41,016,450	73,834,559	1,507,809	77.6
1940	47,686,591	46,482,060	94,168,651	20,334,092	91.9
1941	41,137,164	60,351,000	101,488,164	7,319,513	86.3
1942	41,974,577	57,234,545	99,209,122	2,279,042*	83.0
1943	43,013,495	55,897,808	98,911,303	297,819*	78.8
1944	47,002,979	56,160,583	103,163,562	4,252,259	74.0
1945	54,288,000	59,823,000	114,111,000	10,947,438	71.0

Source: Savings and Loan Annals, 1938–1946.
* Denotes decrease.

TABLE 40

SURPLUS AND UNDIVIDED PROFITS ACCOUNTS OF TEXAS
SAVINGS AND LOAN ASSOCIATIONS, 1937 TO 1945

Year	State	Federal	Total
1937	$5,264,347	$1,696,779	$ 6,961,126
1938	3,935,017	2,468,792	6,403,809
1939	3,000,797	2,919,887	5,920,684
1940	4,425,233	3,501,060	7,926,293
1941	1,849,131	4,836,000	6,685,131
1942	3,780,193	5,593,435	9,373,628
1943	4,244,848	6,398,424	10,643,272
1944	5,338,661	6,448,454	11,787,115
1945	6,349,000	7,345,000	13,694,000

Source: Savings and Loan Annals, 1938–1946.

reserves, but the industry itself was coming to place increasing emphasis upon this part of its operation. During this period, more and more attention was given in league meetings to the needs for greater reserves and liquidity.

Another change during the period from 1937 through 1945 was the shift in the attitude of the industry toward broader problems. As might be expected, during the 1930's, when the industry was fighting for survival, it had little time or inclination to consider much more than the problem of keeping open. For the most part, the industry favored any sort of government assistance which might be expected to strengthen its status. But as times improved, the industry began looking with wonder at many of the government institutions. While the savings and loan industry readily supported the Home Loan Bank and the Federal Savings and Loan Insurance Corporation, it became less enthusiastic about the Federal Housing Administration and openly hostile toward public housing. One illustration of this attitude, which became pronounced at the end of this period, can be found in the following speech made by Walter McAllister[2] of San Antonio before the annual meeting of the United States Savings and Loan League in 1945:

No amount of wishful thinking can isolate our business from economic or political trends. The great struggle now well advanced is between private free enterprise and planned economy. . . . Many savings and loan executives clearly see the dangers to our American way of life. Every session of Congress observes Government making further inroads into what has been the field of private endeavor. Our individual freedom is being constantly constricted and in no field of our economy is the progress of Socialism or Statism more apparent than in the activities of the public housers.[3]

While that statement is not necessarily characteristic of the industry, it does indicate a growing sentiment among savings and loan people against government activity. This is especially significant, as the industry, particularly because of its previous tax exemptions, has been referred to as a government-subsidized one. While there may possibly have been a time when the industry favored government subsidy, by the end of this period it no longer did so.

In line with this change in attitude, the period saw the cessation of the trend toward converting to federal charters. In 1937 there were eighty-seven state associations and eighty-nine federals in Texas. The year 1937 was the first one in which the number of federal associations exceeded the number of state associations in Texas. For a while it appeared that the federal associations would come to dominate the field. As is shown in Table 35, the number of state associations declined to a low of fifty in 1943, but the trend then

[2] In 1953, Walter W. McAllister was appointed by President Eisenhower to the position of Chairman of the Home Loan Bank Board, a position he holds at the present time.

[3] Walter W. McAllister, "The Work and Opportunities of the Savings and Loan Business in the Next Ten Years," *Savings and Loan Annals, 1945* (Chicago: United States Savings and Loan League, 1946), pp. 260–261.

reversed itself, and the number of state associations began to increase as the number of federal associations declined. By 1945 the number of federal associations still exceeded the number of state associations by thirty-five, but the trend was again toward an increase in the state associations.

Balance sheets for the years 1937 through 1945 (with the exception of 1939 and 1940, the years for which no reports were prepared by the Department of Banking) are presented on the following pages.

TABLE 41

CONSOLIDATED STATEMENT OF CONDITION OF STATE SAVINGS AND LOAN ASSOCIATIONS IN TEXAS, DECEMBER 31, 1937

Texas associations (87)

Assets

First mortgage and other loans	$43,147,873.46
Real estate owned and sold on contract	12,044,696.90
Stock in Federal Home Loan Bank	246,900.00
U. S. government bonds and other securities	1,037,165.87
Cash on hand and in banks	1,950,225.23
Office buildings (net)	543,561.15
Furniture and fixtures (net)	90,306.00
Other assets	469,327.43
Total assets	$59,530,001.04

Liabilities

Free or repurchasable shares	$44,254,903.52
Mortgage pledged shares	3,732,784.72
Advances and borrowed money	3,886,225.95
Advance payments by borrowers for taxes and insurance	139,990.32
Dividends declared and unpaid	291,496.23
Other liabilities	675,042.43
Permanent reserve or guaranty stock	1,238,535.79
Reserves and undivided profits	5,311,022.08
Total liabilities	$59,530,001.04
Foreign associations (3) assets	$33,416,528.45
Federal associations (89) assets	$24,186,152.00

Source: Ninth Annual Report of Building and Loan Associations, 1937, pp. 2–3.
Note: The domestic assets in the above balance sheet do not add up to the total shown; however, they are reproduced as found in the annual report.

TABLE 42

CONSOLIDATED STATEMENT OF CONDITION OF STATE SAVINGS AND
LOAN ASSOCIATIONS IN TEXAS, DECEMBER 31, 1938

Texas associations (71)
Assets

First mortgage and other loans	$37,764,795.60
Real estate owned and sold on contract	5,909,258.74
Stock in Federal Home Loan Bank	335,000.00
U. S. government bonds and other securities	168,096.27
Cash on hand and in banks	1,535,401.41
Office buildings (net)	495,355.46
Furniture and fixtures (net)	100,256.73
Other assets	158,780.30
Total assets	$46,466,944.51

Liabilities

Free or repurchasable shares	$35,414,725.11
Mortgage pledged shares	2,792,155.68
Advances and borrowed money	2,764,391.02
Advance payments by borrowers for taxes and insurance	297,076.32
Dividends declared and unpaid	323,304.76
Other liabilities	512,573.78
Permanent reserve or guaranty stock	920,000.00
Reserves and undivided profits	3,442,717.84
Total liabilities	$46,466,944.51
Foreign associations (4) assets	$32,199,494.79

Source: *Tenth Annual Report of Building and Loan Associations, 1938*, pp. 2–3.

TABLE 43

CONSOLIDATED STATEMENT OF CONDITION OF FEDERAL SAVINGS AND
LOAN ASSOCIATIONS IN TEXAS, DECEMBER 31, 1940

Texas associations (91)
Assets

First mortgage loans	$46,481,000.00
Other loans	343,000.00
Real estate sold on contract	1,230,000.00
Real estate owned	594,000.00
Federal Home Loan Bank stock	474,000.00
Other investments	132,000.00
Cash on hand and in banks	4,100,000.00
Office building (net)	335,000.00
Furniture and fixtures (net)	69,000.00
Other assets	56,000.00
Total assets	$53,814,000.00

Liabilities

Savings capital	$46,925,000.00
Mortgaged pledged shares	290,000.00
Advances from Federal Home Loan Bank	1,359,000.00
Other borrowed money	46,000.00
Loans in process	574,000.00
Other liabilities	863,000.00
Deferred credits	73,000.00
Specific reserves	181,000.00
General reserves	2,003,000.00
Undivided profits	1,500,000.00
Total liabilities	$53,814,000.00

Source: Charles M. Torrance, chief, Operating Analysis Division, Home Loan Bank Board, Washington, D.C.

TABLE 44

CONSOLIDATED STATEMENT OF CONDITION OF STATE SAVINGS AND LOAN ASSOCIATIONS IN TEXAS, DECEMBER 31, 1941

Texas associations (52)
Assets

First mortgage and other loans	$ 40,660,056.57
Real estate owned and real estate sold on contract	2,798,153.25
Stock in Federal Home Loan Bank	365,700.00
U.S. government bonds and other securities	532,624.90
Cash on hand and in banks	2,282,742.96
Office buildings (net)	554,096.74
Furniture and fixtures (net)	62,424,81
Other assets	62,841.86
Total assets	$ 47,318,641.09

Liabilities

Free or repurchasable shares	$ 39,684,458.70
Pledged shares	1,227,509.05
Advances and borrowed money	1,657,272.17
Advance payments by borrowers for taxes and insurance	481,473.96
Dividends declared and unpaid	376,393.11
Other liabilities	489,121.73
Permanent reserves or guaranty stock	460,700.00
Reserves and undivided profits	2,941,712.37
Total liabilities	$ 47,318,641.09
Foreign associations (4) assets	$38,837,605.13

Source: Fourteenth Annual Report of Savings, Building and Loan Associations, 1942, pp. 2–7.

TABLE 45

CONSOLIDATED STATEMENT OF CONDITION OF FEDERAL SAVINGS AND
LOAN ASSOCIATIONS IN TEXAS, DECEMBER 31, 1941

Texas associations (92)

Assets

First mortgage loans	$ 60,330,000.00
Other loans	354,000.00
Real estate sold on contract	1,153,000.00
Real estate owned	504,000.00
Federal Home Loan Bank stock	605,000.00
U.S. government obligations	422,000.00
Other investments	15,000.00
Cash on hand and in banks	4,300,000.00
Office building (net)	351,000.00
Furniture and fixtures (net)	95,000.00
Other assets	57,000.00
Total assets	$ 68,186,000.00

Liabilities

Savings capital	$ 58,034,000.00
Mortgaged pledged shares	321,000.00
Advances from Federal Home Loan Bank	2,879,000.00
Other borrowed money	42,000.00
Loans in process	690,000.00
Other liabilities	1,100,000.00
Deferred credits	68,000.00
Specific reserves	216,000.00
General reserves	2,885,000.00
Undivided profits	1,951,000.00
Total liabilities	$ 68,186,000.00

Source: Charles M. Torrance, chief, Operating Analysis Division, Home Loan Bank Board, Washington, D.C.

TABLE 46

CONSOLIDATED STATEMENT OF CONDITION OF STATE SAVINGS AND
LOAN ASSOCIATIONS IN TEXAS, DECEMBER 31, 1942

Texas associations (52)

Assets

First mortgage and other loans	$ 42,355,715.47
Real estate owned and sold on contract	2,283,519.23
Stock in Federal Home Loan Bank	395,300.00
U.S. government bonds and other securities	2,072,490.41
Cash on hand and in banks	2,578,875.28
Office buildings (net)	538,136.42
Furniture and fixtures (net)	56,434.66
Other assets	210,224.46
Total assets	$ 50,490,695.93

Liabilities

Free or repurchasable shares	$ 42,950,705.88
Mortgage pledged shares	1,056,062.35
Advances and borrowed money	1,237,969.59
Advance payments by borrowers for taxes and insurance	535,535.05
Dividends declared and unpaid	378,139.77
Other liabilities	430,139.16
Permanent reserve or guaranty stock	460,700.00
Reserves and undivided profits	3,441,444.13
Total liabilities	$ 50,490,695.93
Foreign associations (3) assets	$39,598,538.92

Source: Fourteenth Annual Report of Building and Loan Associations, 1942, pp. 2–3.

TABLE 47

CONSOLIDATED STATEMENT OF CONDITION OF FEDERAL SAVINGS AND
LOAN ASSOCIATIONS IN TEXAS, DECEMBER 31, 1942

Texas associations (92)

Assets

First mortgage loans	$57,235,000.00
Other loans	189,000.00
Real estate sold on contract	972,000.00
Real estate owned	262,000.00
Federal Home Loan Bank stock	642,000.00
U.S. government obligations	3,479,000.00
Other investments	48,000.00
Cash on hand and in banks	5,673,000.00
Office building (net)	352,000.00
Furniture and fixtures (net)	92,000.00
Other assets	49,000.00
Total assets	$68,993,000.00

Liabilities

Savings capital	$61,165,000.00
Mortgage pledged shares	198,000.00
Advances from Federal Home Loan Bank	479,000.00
Other borrowed money	9,000.00
Loans in process	116,000.00
Other liabilities	1,161,000.00
Deferred credits	87,000.00
Specific reserves	199,000.00
General reserves	3,270,000.00
Undivided profits	2,309,000.00
Total liabilities	$68,993,000.00

Source: Charles M. Torrance, chief, Operating Analysis Division, Home Loan Bank Board, Washington, D.C.

TABLE 48

CONSOLIDATED STATEMENT OF CONDITION OF STATE SAVINGS AND LOAN ASSOCIATIONS IN TEXAS, DECEMBER 31, 1943

Texas associations (50)

Assets

First mortgage loans and short term loans	$43,361,273.98
Real estate owned and real estate sold on contract	1,529,098.62
Stock Federal Home Loan Bank	441,400.00
U.S. government bonds and securities	5,349,145.97
Cash on hand and in banks	2,711,339.98
Office building	525,070.82
Furniture and fixtures	51,699.03
Other assets	44,282.01
Total assets	$54,013,310.41

Liabilities

Share Accounts:

Free	$46,812,995.68
Pledged	779,310.56
Advances and borrowed money	797,814.95
Advance payments by borrowers	574,607.55
Dividends declared and unpaid	321,462.78
Permanent reserve or guaranty stock	460,700.00
Other liabilities	319,958.66
Reserves and undivided profits	3,946,460.23
Total liabilities	$54,013,310.41
Foreign associations (3) assets	$45,153,393.33

Source: Fifteenth Annual Report of Savings, Building and Loan Associations, 1943.

TABLE 49

CONSOLIDATED STATEMENT OF CONDITION OF FEDERAL SAVINGS AND
LOAN ASSOCIATIONS IN TEXAS, DECEMBER 31, 1943

Texas associations (92)
Assets

First mortgage loans	$ 55,898,000.00
Other loans	154,000.00
Real estate sold on contract	705,000.00
Real estate owned	104,000.00
Federal Home Loan Bank stock	652,000.00
U. S. government obligations	8,226,000.00
Other investments	33,000.00
Cash on hand and in banks	5,236,000.00
Office building (net)	373,000.00
Furniture and fixtures (net)	80,000.00
Other assets	55,000.00
Total assets	$ 71,516,000.00

Liabilities

Savings capital	$ 62,414,000.00
Mortgage pledged shares	119,000.00
Advances from Federal Home Loan Bank	903,000.00
Other borrowed money	115,000.00
Loans in process	244,000.00
Other liabilities	1,089,000.00
Deferred credits	80,000.00
Specific reserves	187,000.00
General reserves	3,787,000.00
Undivided profits	2,578,000.00
Total liabilities	$ 71,516,000.00

Source: Charles M. Torrance, chief, Operating Analysis Division, Home Loan Bank Board, Washington, D.C.

TABLE 50

CONSOLIDATED STATEMENT OF CONDITION OF STATE SAVINGS AND LOAN ASSOCIATIONS IN TEXAS, DECEMBER 31, 1944

Texas associations (51)

Assets

First mortgage loans and short term loans	$ 47,002,978.52
Real estate owned and sold on contract	1,077,903.04
Stock Federal Home Loan Bank	471,300.00
U. S. government bonds and securities	10,090,950.64
Cash on hand and in banks	3,271,277.12
Office building	553,659.92
Furniture and fixtures	40,027.20
Other assets	90,168.03
Total assets	$ 62,598,264.47

Liabilities

Share Accounts:

Free	$ 53,525,908.23
Pledged	620,806.19
Advances and borrowed money	1,220,862.41
Advance payments by borrowers	668,248.80
Dividends declared and unpaid	336,849.64
Permanent reserve or guaranty stock	630,700.00
Other liabilities	256,227.86
Reserves and undivided profits	5,338,661.34
Total liabilities	$ 62,598,264.47
Foreign associations (2) assets	$46,512,008.25

Source: Sixteenth Annual Report of Savings, Building and Loan Associations, 1944, pp. 5–8.

TABLE 51

CONSOLIDATED STATEMENT OF CONDITION OF FEDERAL SAVINGS AND
LOAN ASSOCIATIONS IN TEXAS, DECEMBER 31, 1944

Texas associations (90)

Assets

First mortgage loans	$ 56,160,000.00
Other loans	123,000.00
Real estate sold on contract	501,000.00
Real estate owned	76,000.00
Federal Home Loan Bank stock	637,000.00
U. S. government obligations	14,625,000.00
Other investments	54,000.00
Cash on hand and in banks	3,943,000.00
Office building (net)	532,000.00
Furniture and fixtures (net)	58,000.00
Other assets	45,000.00
Total assets	$ 76,754,000.00

Liabilities

Savings capital	$ 67,099,000.00
Mortgage pledged shares	60,000.00
Advances from Federal Home Loan Bank	876,000.00
Other borrowed money	727,000.00
Loans in process	262,000.00
Other liabilities	1,051,000.00
Deferred credits	53,000.00
Specific reserves	177,000.00
General reserves	4,131,000.00
Undivided profits	2,318,000.00
Total liabilities	$ 76,754,000.00

Source: Charles M. Torrance, chief, Operating Analysis Division, Home Loan Bank Board, Washington, D.C.

TABLE 52

CONSOLIDATED STATEMENT OF CONDITION OF STATE SAVINGS AND
LOAN ASSOCIATIONS IN TEXAS, DECEMBER 31, 1945

Texas associations (54)

Assets

First mortgage and other loans	$ 54,287,770.15
Real estate owned and real estate sold on contract	583,924.47
Stock in Federal Home Loan Banks	534,100.00
U. S. government bonds and other securities	16,374,158.90
Cash on hand and in banks	2,850,352.19
Office buildings (net)	703,593.35
Furniture and fixtures (net)	31,938.87
Other assets	81,508.44
Total assets	$ 75,447,346.37

Liabilities

Free or repurchasable shares	$ 63,020,672.24
Pledged shares	556,952.95
Advances and borrowed money	3,643,604.96
Advance payments by borrowers for taxes and insurance	541,793.42
Dividends declared and unpaid	442,907.88
Other liabilities	891,914.82
Permanent reserve or guaranty stock	773,200.00
Reserves and undivided profits	5,576,300.00
Total liabilities	$ 75,447,346.37
Foreign associations (2) assets	$53,017,940.90

Source: Seventeenth Annual Report of Savings, Building and Loan Associations, 1945, p. 3.

TABLE 53

CONSOLIDATED STATEMENT OF CONDITION OF FEDERAL SAVINGS AND
LOAN ASSOCIATIONS IN TEXAS, DECEMBER 31, 1945

Texas associations (87)

Assets

First mortgage loans	$ 59,823,000.00
Other loans (including share loans)	165,000.00
Real estate sold on contract	333,000.00
Real estate owned	58,000.00
Federal Home Loan Bank stock	675,000.00
U. S. government obligations	19,317,000.00
Other investments (including accrued interest)	57,000.00
Cash on hand and in banks	4,209,000.00
Office building (net)	522,000.00
Furniture, fixtures and equipment (net)	54,000.00
Other assets	73,000.00
Total assets	$ 85,286,000.00

Liabilities

U. S. government investment	$ 74,000.00
Private repurchasable capital	72,257,000.00
Mortgage pledged shares	53,000.00
Advances from Federal Home Loan Bank	1,622,000.00
Other borrowed money	2,095,000.00
Loans in process	980,000.00
Other liabilities	616,000.00
Deferred credits	52,000.00
Specific reserves	191,000.00
General reserves	4,567,000.00
Undivided profits	2,779,000.00
Total liabilities	$ 85,286,000.00

*Source: Annual Report, Combined Financial Statements of Members of the Federal Home Loan Bank System,
1945, Washington, D.C.*
*Note: The domestic assets in the above balance sheet do not add up to the total shown; however, they are
reproduced as found in the annual report.*

The Period 1946–1953

Because this period—1946 through 1953—covers the most recent stage in the history of savings and loan associations in Texas, it will be discussed in greater detail than were the prior periods and will deal with three main topics: (1) the changes in the savings and loan industry from 1946 through 1953, (2) the status of the industry at the end of 1953, and (3) the procedure followed by the Savings, Building and Loan Supervisor of Texas in chartering new associations.

Changes in the Savings and Loan Industry, 1946–1953

In many respects the period from 1946 to 1953 is the most interesting period of savings and loan history in Texas. Within those years Texas enjoyed the highest level of building activity in its history, and the savings and loan associations in the state experienced a corresponding growth. In 1946 there were fifty-one state associations, with total assets of $96,034,-921.43. In 1953 there were eighty-four domestic associations, which owned assets of $380,990,391.99. Probably more significant than the actual number of associations is the fact that in 1953, for the first time since 1936, the number of state-chartered associations exceeded those with federal charters. This situation continued after 1953.

Many facts help explain the conversion from federal to state charters. Part of the change can be clarified by a review of the reasons why state associations originally converted to federals. Some converted for added prestige which might be expected to accompany a federal charter, others to expedite obtaining insurance coverage or for assistance which it was hoped might be more readily available to federal associations. When it was found either that

TABLE 54

NUMBER OF SAVINGS AND LOAN ASSOCIATIONS OPERATING IN TEXAS,
BY TYPE, 1946 TO 1953

Year	State	Federal	Foreign	Total
1946	51	86	2	139
1947	54	86	2	142
1948	57	85	1	143
1949	57	84	1	142
1950	62	83	1	146
1951	68	83	1	152
1952	77	82	1	160
1953	84	80	1	165

Source: *Annual Report of Savings and Loan Associations in Texas, 1946–1953. Combined Financial Statements, Members of the Home Loan Bank System, 1946–1953.*

a federal charter did not bring additional prestige or that the need for additional prestige was not as great, the desirability of a federal charter declined. Also, insurance from the Federal Savings and Loan Insurance Corporation and membership in the Home Loan Bank System is now as readily available to state as to federal associations.

Perhaps the most important advantage to be claimed for state associations is that they are allowed to have permanent stock. In fact, the State Savings, Building and Loan Supervisor will not permit the organization of an association at the present time unless there are provisions for permanent stock. Permanent stock is sought because of the greater security which goes with its ownership. Inasmuch as it is not customarily so widely diffused as repurchasable stock, it makes control easier. Further, the by-laws can be so drafted as to restrict either a majority or all of the board of directors to holders of permanent stock. While all members or shareholders of an association must be given the right to vote, the use of permanent stock effectively limits the ones for whom they can vote. It is true that the use of proxies in associations without permanent stock assures management, in most instances, that it will retain control, but there is always the possibility at least that loss of control will occur.

A permanent stock plan is desirable for other reasons as well. There is no requirement that permanent stockholders be paid the same dividend that other investors receive. Promoters and organizers of savings and loan associations often put large amounts of their own time, effort, and money into an association. While they may not expect immediate compensation, if the association is successful, permanent stock may be considered a reward for the additional risks assumed. Permanent stock has desirable traits if a transfer is anticipated. While an officer, director, or other prominent owner of stock in an association can transfer any type of share by gift, sale, bequest, or other means, unless the recipient is a part of the existing management, the transferer does not transfer the other advantages which went with his stock ownership. Thus, the new owner will receive no better treatment than ordinary shareholders. If the stock is permanent stock, the recipient is more likely to obtain preferential treatment, either in the matter of dividends or by being given some other consideration. This feature is especially important if the present owner of stock wishes his heirs to receive the maximum benefit from stock which he currently owns; even though the heirs themselves may not wish to enter the business.

Another reason for an increase in state-chartered associations is that many savings and loan people believe that local regulation, by virtue of its proximity, is better able to deal with the problems which occur locally. This reason is offset somewhat by the existence of eleven district Federal Home

Loan Banks, the regulatory and supervisory agencies. Since these banks are in close contact with their members, they are able, in many instances, to care for local problems. Many businessmen seem to believe, however, that local regulation is preferable to federal regulation and that state regulatory agencies are more responsive to the desires of their constituents than are national ones.

The final reason that state incorporation may be more desirable than federal is that the state associations in Texas are given greater latitude in the

TABLE 55

TOTAL ASSETS OF TEXAS SAVINGS AND LOAN ASSOCIATIONS, 1946 TO 1953
(in thousands of dollars)

Year	State	Federal	Total	Increase of total assets over previous year
1946	96,035	103,509	199,544	....
1947	113,478	123,527	237,005	37,461
1948	131,995	143,657	275,652	38,647
1949	155,892	166,831	322,723	47,071
1950	191,465	198,916	390,381	67,658
1951	227,295	233,730	461,025	70,644
1952	289,719	276,689	566,408	105,383
1953	380,990	332,419	713,409	147,001

Source: *Annual Report of Savings and Loan Associations in Texas, 1946–1953. Combined Financial Statements, Members of the Home Loan Bank System, 1946–1953.*

nature of loans and investments which they may make. State associations are allowed a certain amount of personal loan business and are not restricted in their investment activities to government bonds.

During the period under consideration, 1946 through 1953, the number and proportion of state associations which became members of the Home Loan Bank System increased. In 1945 state member associations owned assets of $91,996,303, less than 96 percent of the total assets of state associations. By 1953 the assets of state member associations had increased to $374,-213,000, which represented more than 98 percent of the total assets of state associations. Numberwise, the increase in membership was even greater. In 1946, as seen in Table 56, there were 37 member associations. These represented slightly more than 72 percent of the total state associations. By 1953 the number of state member associations had increased to 74, approximately 89 percent of all the state associations. As explained later in this chapter, no new nonmember associations are being organized.

An analysis of balance sheet items of Texas savings and loan associations reveals that the amount of cash and government securities increased substantially from 1946 to 1953, but the ratio of cash and government securities to total assets declined. During the same period, the percentage of loans to total assets increased. Both these developments indicate favorable times for savings and loan operation. While there are exceptions in specific years, the federal associations generally hold a higher percentage of their assets in the form of cash and government securities and a lower percentage in loans than do the state associations.

TABLE 56

STATE ASSOCIATIONS OPERATING IN TEXAS, 1946 TO 1953

Year	Members	Insured	Nonmembers	Uninsured	Total
1946	37	33	14	18	51
1947	38	34	16	20	54
1948	42	38	15	19	57
1949	46	42	11	15	57
1950	51	47	11	15	62
1951	54	51	14	17	68
1952	60	57	16	19	76
1953	74	71	10	13	84

Source: *Annual Report of Savings and Loan Associations in Texas, 1946–1953. Combined Financial Statements, Members of the Home Loan Bank System, 1946–1953.*

Present Status of the Savings and Loan Industry in Texas

State-chartered savings and loan associations in Texas are supervised by the Commissioner of Banking. However, as mentioned in Chapter IV, the Forty-sixth Legislature in 1939 passed Senate Bill No. 13, which made provisions for appointment of a Building and Loan Supervisor—the title was subsequently changed to Savings, Building and Loan Supervisor—who has immediate regulatory powers.

The Savings, Building and Loan Supervisor is under the direction of the Banking Commissioner of Texas and is responsible to the Commissioner. The law requires that the Supervisor, before his appointment, must have had experience in a savings and loan association and also as a savings and loan examiner.

The average size of state associations was somewhat greater than that of the federal associations in 1953. For state associations the average size was approximately $4,534,000; for the federals it was approximately $4,155,000. In 1953, 54 state associations, approximately 62 percent, had assets of less than $3 million. Though the percentage of state associations with assets of less than $3 million is very little more than for federal associations, one would expect the opposite, inasmuch as the average size of the state associations is greater. This can be explained primarily by the relatively larger proportion of new, hence smaller, associations with state charters. Eight state associations were organized in both 1952 and 1953. Most of the associations in the state had assets of less than $10 million in 1953, 86 percent of the state associations and 89 percent of the federal. The largest association in Texas was a state association with assets of $43,473,200.98.

Savings and loan activity in Texas, compared with that in other states, is high. With 154 member associations in 1953, Texas ranked sixth in the nation in the number of member associations, the same rank it holds in population. However, by other criteria, it does not rank this high. Measured by total mortgage loans and total assets in insured associations, Texas, with mortgage loans of $577,584,000 and assets of $705,450,000, ranked ninth. This can be explained by the large geographic area. Savings and loan associations are mostly local institutions, hence there tends to be a relatively large number of them in sparsely populated areas.

The year 1953 was one of great increase in savings capital in insured associations in Texas. During the year these associations showed an increase of $244,678,000, which, when compared with increases in other states, also ranked ninth.

By conservative standards, the savings and loan associations in Texas seem to rank ninth, obviously a high place. It is true that Texas does not have some of the institutions which most strongly compete with savings and loan associations, namely, savings banks or mutuals. Measured by the test used above, however, institutions which are members of the Federal Home Loan Bank System and insured by the Federal Savings and Loan Insurance Corporation, the inclusion of these other institutions would not alter the rank assigned to Texas.[4]

Requirements for Organizing a New State-Chartered Association

The legal requirements for chartering an association under Texas law have been discussed in Chapter IV. In addition to the legal requirements, the State Banking Commissioner and the Savings and Loan Supervisor enforce extralegal requirements which, in effect, constitute the present requirements for organizing an association in Texas.

The first test to which the Building and Loan Supervisor submits a proposed association is that of need. While we have "free" chartering of savings and loan associations in the state, administrative action has the effect of

---

[4] *Savings and Home Financing Source Book, 1954* (Washington, D.C.: Housing and Home Finance Agency, 1954), pp. 10–11.

limiting the number of associations. In this respect, the situation is similar to the one which prevails in commercial banking. Although in recent years there have been more savings and loan associations chartered than there have been commercial banks,[5] this may be explained by the fact that the savings and loan industry is a newer one, and thus the field is not so near saturation as is commercial banking. It does not appear to represent weaker control by the Savings, Building and Loan Supervisor.

Need, as interpreted by the Savings, Building and Loan Supervisor, differs somewhat from the usual connotation of the word. A need exists if the situation is such as reasonably to assure the success of the proposed association. The Supervisor is influenced by such factors as existing savings and loan facilities and the level of economic activity in the area the proposed association will serve. And he considers not only the need for an association as a lender of mortgage funds, but also the need for an association to serve investors. Unless there is reason to believe that a large proportion of both the demand for mortgage funds and the supply of loanable funds can be obtained locally, the Supervisor will be inclined to conclude that insufficient need exists to warrant the organization of an association. The result of this approach has been to prevent the organization of many proposed associations and to strengthen the industry.

A proposed association at the present time must be a permanent stock association. A mutual, or nonpermanent, stock association has not been chartered in Texas since World War II. The minimum amount of permanent stock which will be approved is $75,000 plus a paid-in reserve of at least 25 percent. This is customarily accomplished by selling the permanent stock at $125 a share, with $100 going to permanent stock and $25 to surplus. If the proposed association is to be in or near a large city, the amount of permanent stock and surplus required will be larger. There have been instances in which a proposed application for charter was not approved until the organization agreed to provide a paid-in surplus equal to 50 percent of the permanent stock. The surplus is expected to be available, if needed, to pay the cost of operation during the early years. In areas, usually large cities, where rents and advertising costs are high and the scale of contemplated operation is large enough to require well-trained, expensive management, higher reserves will be required.

Permanent stock, once issued, is not subject to repurchase by the association. It is not insurable and cannot be pledged as security for loans. An association cannot pay a dividend on permanent stock for the first three years of operation. The Savings, Building and Loan Supervisor will not issue a

[5] From 1950 through 1953 Texas chartered 17 new commercial banks and 25 new savings and loan associations.

charter until the Federal Savings and Loan Insurance Corporation agrees
to insure the association. While there are some associations in the state which
are members of the Home Loan Bank but do not have insurance, no new
associations are allowed to become members without obtaining insurance.[6]

Before granting a charter, the Savings, Building and Loan Supervisor
visits the town in which the association plans to operate. This is done not
only to meet the organizers but also to obtain an accurate picture of the local
environment, public attitudes, and attitude of the existing banking interests
and to learn other pertinent facts which might influence his decision. The
Commissioner, in effect, uses the chartering activity as the first step in supervision and regulation.

If the level of economic activity continues to increase in Texas, as most
forecasters expect, there will be increased business for savings and loan associations. This does not necessarily mean that a proportionately larger number of savings and loan associations will be needed to handle the increased
business which should be forthcoming. Judging by the current practices
employed in chartering new institutions, it seems likely that most new associations will be chartered either in areas not currently being served by an
association or in areas which have grown at a disproportionally rapid rate
and are not adequately served by existing associations. The effect of the
supervisor's current policy can be expected to result in stronger, but not
necessarily many more, associations. Judging by past experience, this is a
desirable development.

The following pages present consolidated balance sheets of Texas associations from 1946 through 1953.

[6] At the present time there are two noninsured member associations in Texas.

TABLE 57

CONSOLIDATED STATEMENT OF CONDITION OF STATE SAVINGS AND
LOAN ASSOCIATIONS IN TEXAS, DECEMBER 31, 1946

Texas associations (51)
Assets

First mortgage and other loans	$ 78,190,863.00
Real estate owned and sold on contract	354,064.43
Stock in Federal Home Loan Bank	751,700.00
U. S. government bonds and other securities	12,736,332.50
Cash on hand and in banks	3,141,531.35
Office building less depreciation	718,412.54
Furniture and fixtures less depreciation	40,003.08
Other assets	102,014.53
Total assets	$ 96,034,921.43

Liabilities

Free or repurchasable shares	$ 78,317,336.76
Pledged shares	499,452.50
Advances and borrowed money	6,626,516.91
Advance payments by borrowers for taxes and insurance	567,967.13
Dividends declared and unpaid	612,664.48
Other liabilities	1,642,582.09
Permanent reserve or guaranty stock	1,133,017.00
Reserve and undivided profits	6,635,384.56
Total liabilities	$ 96,034,921.43
Foreign associations (2) assets	$60,926,311.74

Source: *Eighteenth Annual Report of Savings, Building and Loan Associations, 1946.*

TABLE 58

CONSOLIDATED STATEMENT OF CONDITION OF FEDERAL SAVINGS AND
LOAN ASSOCIATIONS IN TEXAS, DECEMBER 31, 1946

Texas associations (51)
Assets

First mortgage loans	$ 83,361,000.00
Other loans	196,000.00
Real estate sold on contract	197,000.00
Real estate owned	9,000.00
Federal Home Loan Bank stock	780,000.00
U. S. government obligations	13,369,000.00
Other investments	39,000.00
Cash	5,018,000.00
Office building	330,000.00
Furniture and fixtures	60,000.00
Other assets	151,000.00
Total assets	$103,510,000.00

Liabilities

U. S. government shares	$ 55,000.00
Savings capital	86,399,000.00
Mortgage pledged shares	25,000.00
Advances from Federal Home Loan Bank	4,244,000.00
Borrowed money	2,416,000.00
Loans in process	1,279,000.00
Other liabilities	1,090,000.00
Deferred credits	49,000.00
Specific reserves	269,000.00
General reserves	4,996,000.00
Undivided profits	2,688,000.00
Total liabilities	$103,510,000.00

Source: Annual Report, Combined Financial Statements of Members of the Federal Home Loan Bank System, 1946, Washington, D.C.

TABLE 59

CONSOLIDATED STATEMENT OF CONDITION OF STATE SAVINGS AND
LOAN ASSOCIATIONS IN TEXAS, DECEMBER 31, 1947

Texas associations (54)

Assets

First mortgage and other loans	$ 96,073,465.89
Real estate owned and sold on contract	248,363.21
Stock in Federal Home Loan Bank	862,100.00
U. S. government bonds and other securities	11,727,801.47
Cash on hand and in banks	3,558,985.39
Office building less depreciation	871,769.86
Furniture and fixtures less depreciation	58,548.85
Other assets	76,663.69
Total assets	$113,477,698.36

Liabilities

Free or repurchasable shares	$ 91,943,012.92
Pledged shares	665,946.07
Advances and borrowed money	8,798,410.37
Advance payments by borrowers for taxes and insurance	657,338.61
Dividends declared and unpaid	654,426.39
Other liabilities	1,643,216.36
Permanent reserve or guaranty stock	1,304,600.00
Reserve and undivided profits	7,810,747.64
Total liabilities	$113,477,698.36
Foreign associations (2) assets	$68,916,823.86

Source: Nineteenth Annual Report of Savings, Building and Loan Associations, 1947.

TABLE 60

CONSOLIDATED STATEMENT OF CONDITION OF FEDERAL SAVINGS AND
LOAN ASSOCIATIONS IN TEXAS, DECEMBER 31, 1947

Texas associations (86)

Assets

First mortgage loans	$103,657,000.00
Other loans (including share loans)	335,000.00
Real estate sold on contract	149,000.00
Real estate owned	6,000.00
Federal Home Loan Bank stock	975,000.00
U. S. government obligations	11,891,000.00
Other investments (including accrued interest)	27,000.00
Cash on hand and in banks	5,641,000.00
Office building (net)	674,000.00
Furniture, fixtures and equipment (net)	70,000.00
Other assets	102,000.00
Total assets	$123,527,000.00

Liabilities

U. S. government investment	$ 49,000.00
Private repurchasable capital	105,277,000.00
Mortgage pledged shares	26,000.00
Advances from Federal Home Loan Bank	5,316,000.00
Other borrowed money	990,000.00
Loans in process	1,280,000.00
Other liabilities	1,034,000.00
Permanent, reserve or guaranty stock	
Deferred credits	53,000.00
Specific reserves	269,000.00
General reserves	6,175,000.00
Undivided profits	3,058,000.00
Total liabilities	$123,527,000.00

Source: Annual Report, Combined Financial Statements of Members of the Federal Home Loan Bank System, 1947, Washington, D.C.

TABLE 61

CONSOLIDATED STATEMENT OF CONDITION OF STATE SAVINGS AND
LOAN ASSOCIATIONS IN TEXAS, DECEMBER 31, 1948

Texas associations (57)

Assets

First mortgage and other loans	$113,894,692.12
Real estate owned and sold on contract	186,777.09
Stock in Federal Home Loan Bank	1,025,200.00
U. S. government bonds and other securities	10,350,086.65
Cash on hand and in banks	5,255,667.05
Office building less depreciation	1,119,262.73
Furniture and fixtures less depreciation	93,035.81
Other assets	69,990.68
Total assets	$131,994,712.13

Liabilities

Free or repurchasable shares	$109,616,445.87
Pledged shares	829,650.67
Advances and borrowed money	7,761,306.86
Advance payments by borrowers for taxes and insurance	847,662.36
Dividends declared and unpaid	910,177.18
Other liabilities	1,383,446.17
Permanent reserves or guaranty stock	1,680,055.00
Reserves and undivided profits	8,965,968.02
Total liabilities	$131,994,712.13
Foreign association (1)	assets $52,051,089.51

Source: *Twentieth Annual Report of Savings, Building and Loan Associations, 1948*, p. 3.

TABLE 62

CONSOLIDATED STATEMENT OF CONDITION OF FEDERAL SAVINGS AND LOAN ASSOCIATIONS IN TEXAS, DECEMBER 31, 1948

Texas associations (85)
Assets

First mortgage loans	$121,493,000.00
Other loans	678,000.00
Real estate sold on contract	97,000.00
Real estate owned	18,000.00
Federal Home Loan Bank stock	1,150,000.00
U. S. government obligations	11,761,000.00
Other investments (including accrued interest)	32,000.00
Cash on hand and in banks	7,411,000.00
Office building (net)	829,000.00
Furniture, fixtures and equipment (net)	102,000.00
Other assets	86,000.00
Total assets	$143,657,000.00

Liabilities

Savings capital	$124,213,000.00
Mortgage pledged shares	13,000.00
Advances from Federal Home Loan Bank	5,218,000.00
Other borrowed money	1,243,000.00
Loans in process	1,014,000.00
Other liabilities	1,594,000.00
Permanent, reserve or guaranty stock	
Deferred credits	46,000.00
Specific reserves	241,000.00
General reserves	6,927,000.00
Undivided profits	3,148,000.00
Total liabilities	$143,657,000.00

Source: Annual Report, Combined Financial Statements of Members of the Federal Home Loan Bank System, 1948, Washington, D.C.

TABLE 63

CONSOLIDATED STATEMENT OF CONDITION OF STATE SAVINGS AND
LOAN ASSOCIATIONS IN TEXAS, DECEMBER 31, 1949

Texas associations (62)
Assets

First mortgage and other loans	$133,270,070.63
Real estate owned and sold on contract	140,970.57
Stock in Federal Home Loan Bank	1,370,700.00
U. S. government bonds and other securities	11,669,718.38
Cash on hand and in banks	7,781,660.08
Office building less depreciation	1,319,230.23
Furniture and fixtures less depreciation	151,793.17
Other assets	188,232.07
Total assets	$155,892,375.13

Liabilities

Free or repurchasable shares	$132,729,764.25
Pledged shares	784,945.00
Advances and borrowed money	6,167,361.24
Advance payments by borrowers for taxes and insurance	929,520.26
Dividends declared and unpaid	1,045,980.53
Other liabilities	1,710,048.99
Permanent reserve or guaranty stock	2,318,176.25
Reserves and undivided profits	10,206,578.61
Total liabilities	$155,892,375.13
Foreign association (1) assets	$56,849,531.62

Source: Twenty-first Annual Report of Savings, Building and Loan Associations, 1949, p. 3.

TABLE 64

CONSOLIDATED STATEMENT OF CONDITION OF FEDERAL SAVINGS AND
LOAN ASSOCIATIONS IN TEXAS, DECEMBER 31, 1949

Texas associations (84)
Assets

First mortgage loans	$139,195,000.00
Other loans	1,105,000.00
Real estate sold on contract	94,000.00
Real estate owned	9,000.00
Federal Home Loan Bank stock	1,330,000.00
U. S. government obligations	13,383,000.00
Other investments	47,000.00
Cash on hand and in banks	10,103,000.00
Office building (net)	1,243,000.00
Furniture and fixtures (net)	155,000.00
Other assets	167,000.00
Total assets	$166,831,000.00

Liabilities

Savings capital	$147,038,000.00
Mortgage pledged shares	1,000.00
Advances from Federal Home Loan Bank	3,586,000.00
Other borrowed money	931,000.00
Loans in process	1,487,000.00
Other liabilities	1,771,000.00
Permanent stock	
Deferred credits	70,000.00
Specific reserves	306,000.00
General reserves	7,872,000.00
Undivided profits	3,769,000.00
Total liabilities	$166,831,000.00

Source: Annual Report, Combined Financial Statements of Members of the Federal Home Loan Bank System, 1949, Washington, D.C.

TABLE 65

CONSOLIDATED STATEMENT OF CONDITION OF STATE SAVINGS AND
LOAN ASSOCIATIONS IN TEXAS, DECEMBER 31, 1950

Texas associations (63)
Assets

First mortgage and other loans	$165,737,615.14
Real estate owned and sold on contract	134,545.53
Stock in Federal Home Loan Bank	1,576,800.00
U. S. government bonds and other securities	12,786,333.73
Cash on hand and in banks	9,357,659.20
Office building less depreciation	1,516,326.01
Furniture and fixtures less depreciation	220,971.58
Other assets	134,522.41
Total assets	$191,464,773.60

Liabilities

Free or repurchasable shares	$158,086,392.39
Pledged shares	1,012,675.29
Advances and borrowed money	11,964,704.25
Advance payments by borrowers for taxes and insurance	1,382,533.78
Dividends declared and unpaid	1,243,202.39
Other liabilities	2,776,268.60
Permanent reserve or guaranty stock	3,052,176.25
Reserves and undivided profits	11,946,820.65
Total liabilities	$191,464,773.60
Foreign association (1)	assets $62,211,443.07

Source: *Twenty-second Annual Report of Savings, Buildings and Loan Associations, 1950,* p. 3.

TABLE 66

CONSOLIDATED STATEMENT OF CONDITION OF FEDERAL SAVINGS AND
LOAN ASSOCIATIONS IN TEXAS, DECEMBER 31, 1950

Texas associations (83)
Assets

First mortgage loans	$167,097,000.00
Other loans	1,959,000.00
Real estate sold on contract	79,000.00
Real estate owned	39,000.00
Federal Home Loan Bank stock	1,653,000.00
U. S. government obligations	14,436,000.00
Other investments	54,000.00
Cash on hand and in banks	11,508,000.00
Office building (net)	1,604,000.00
Furniture and fixtures (net)	260,000.00
Other assets	227,000.00
Total assets	$198,916,000.00

Liabilities

Savings capital	$171,320,000.00
Mortgage pledged shares	
Advances from Federal Home Loan Bank	8,251,000.00
Other borrowed money	1,563,000.00
Loans in process	1,597,000.00
Other liabilities	2,154,000.00
Permanent stock	
Deferred credits	112,000.00
Specific reserves	372,000.00
General reserves	9,879,000.00
Undivided profits	3,668,000.00
Total liabilities	$198,916,000.00

Source: Annual Report, Combined Financial Statements of Members of the Federal Home Loan Bank System, 1950, Washington, D.C.

TABLE 67

CONSOLIDATED STATEMENT OF CONDITION OF STATE SAVINGS AND
LOAN ASSOCIATIONS IN TEXAS, DECEMBER 31, 1951

Texas associations (69)

Assets

First mortgage and other loans	$195,437,359.68
Real estate owned and sold on contract	115,912.52
Stock in Federal Home Loan Bank	3,266,200.00
U. S. government bonds and other securities	15,645,138.51
Cash on hand and in banks	10,246,761.21
Office building, furniture and fixtures, less depreciation	2,335,836.57
Other assets	247,496.66
Total assets	$227,294,705.15

Liabilities

Free or repurchasable shares	$191,158,312.50
Pledged shares	1,093,248.40
Advances and borrowed money	12,747,885.93
Advance payments by borrowers for taxes and insurance	1,661,074.96
Other liabilities	3,499,743.73
Permanent reserve or guaranty stock	3,715,748.25
Reserves and undivided profits	13,418,691.38
Total liabilities	$227,294,705.15
Foreign association (1) assets	$66,727,037.69

Source: Twenty-third Annual Report of Savings, Building and Loan Associations, 1951, p. 3.

CONSOLIDATED STATEMENT OF CONDITION OF FEDERAL SAVINGS AND
LOAN ASSOCIATIONS IN TEXAS, DECEMBER 31, 1951

Texas associations (83)
Assets

First mortgage loans	$195,072,000.00
Other loans	2,009,000.00
Real estate sold on contract	62,000.00
Real estate owned	19,000.00
Federal Home Loan Bank stock	3,506,000.00
U. S. government obligations	16,463,000.00
Other investments	674,000.00
Cash on hand and in banks	13,622,000.00
Office building (net)	1,735,000.00
Furniture and fixtures (net)	348,000.00
Other assets	220,000.00
Total assets	$233,730,000.00

Liabilities

Savings capital	$202,894,000.00
Advances from Federal Home Loan Bank	10,106,000.00
Other borrowed money	415,000.00
Loans in process	1,278,000.00
Other liabilities	2,452,000.00
Permanent stock	
Deferred credits	143,000.00
Specific reserves	421,000.00
General reserves	11,047,000.00
Undivided profits	4,974,000.00
Total liabilities	$233,730,000.00

Source: Annual Report, Combined Financial Statements of Members of the Federal Home Loan Bank System, 1951, Washington, D.C.

TABLE 69

CONSOLIDATED STATEMENT OF CONDITION OF STATE SAVINGS AND LOAN ASSOCIATIONS IN TEXAS, DECEMBER 31, 1952

Texas associations (77)

Assets

First mortgage and other loans	$247,081,060.80
Real estate owned and sold on contract	114,411.88
Stock in Federal Home Loan Bank	3,829,300.00
U. S. government bonds and other securities	19,343,253.06
Cash on hand and in banks	15,689,782.54
Office building, furniture and fixtures less depreciation	3,375,456.50
Other assets	285,851.96
Total assets	$289,719,116.74

Liabilities

Free or repurchasable shares	$251,354,285.37
Pledged shares	974,609.53
Advances and borrowed money	9,266,759.56
Advance payments by borrowers	2,129,957.80
Other liabilities	3,537,586.98
Permanent reserve or guaranty stock	4,733,430.00
Reserves and undivided profits	17,722,487.50
Total liabilities	$289,719,116.74
Foreign association (1) assets	$76,304,664.70

Source: Twenty-fourth Annual Report of Savings, Building and Loan Associations, 1952.

TABLE 70

CONSOLIDATED STATEMENT OF CONDITION OF FEDERAL SAVINGS AND
LOAN ASSOCIATIONS IN TEXAS, DECEMBER 31, 1952

Texas associations (82)
Assets

First mortgage loans	$232,536,000.00
Other loans	2,479,000.00
Real estate sold on contract	69,000.00
Real estate owned	14,000.00
Federal Home Loan Bank stock	3,725,000.00
U. S. government obligations	19,300,000.00
Other investments	285,000.00
Cash on hand and in banks	15,454,000.00
Office building (net)	2,140,000.00
Furniture and fixtures (net)	466,000.00
Other assets	221,000.00
Total assets	$276,689,000.00

Liabilities

Savings capital	$243,510,000.00
Mortgage pledged shares	
Advances from Federal Home Loan Bank	8,238,000.00
Other borrowed money	1,289,000.00
Loans in process	2,009,000.00
Other liabilities	2,529,000.00
Permanent stock	
Deferred credits	231,000.00
Specific reserves	467,000.00
General reserves	13,504,000.00
Undivided profits	4,912,000.00
Total liabilities	$276,689,000.00

Source: Annual Report, Combined Financial Statements of Members of the Federal Home Loan Bank System, 1952, Washington, D.C.

TABLE 71

CONSOLIDATED STATEMENT OF CONDITION OF STATE SAVINGS AND
LOAN ASSOCIATIONS IN TEXAS, DECEMBER 31, 1953

Texas associations (84)
Assets

First mortgage and other loans	$323,096,276.97
Real estate owned and sold on contract	107,692.58
Stock in Federal Home Loan Bank	4,756,800.00
U. S. government bonds and other securities	25,104,866.53
Cash on hand and in banks	23,187,179.50
Office buildings, furniture and fixtures less depreciation	4,350,494.31
Other assets	387,082.10
Total assets	$380,990,391.99

Liabilities

Free or repurchasable shares	$334,075,308.86
Pledged shares	1,420,918.69
Advances and borrowed money	10,665,460.00
Advance payments by borrowers	2,726,117.46
Other liabilities	3,824,937.07
Permanent reserve or guaranty stock	6,461,790.00
Reserves and undivided profits	21,815,859.91
Total liabilities	$380,990,391.99
Foreign association (1) assets	$103,297,551.75

Source: Twenty-fifth Annual Report of Savings, Building and Loan Associations, 1953.

TABLE 72

CONSOLIDATED STATEMENT OF CONDITION OF FEDERAL SAVINGS AND
LOAN ASSOCIATIONS IN TEXAS, DECEMBER 31, 1953

Texas associations (80)

Assets

First mortgage loans	$279,705,000.00
Other loans	2,894,000.00
Real estate sold on contract	100,000.00
Real estate owned	86,000.00
Federal Home Loan Bank stock	4,279,000.00
U. S. government obligations	21,377,000.00
Other investments	684,000.00
Cash on hand and in banks	19,868,000.00
Office building (net)	2,679,000.00
Furniture and fixtures (net)	522,000.00
Other assets	225,000.00
Total assets	$332,419,000.00

Liabilities

Savings capital	$294,838,000.00
Mortgage pledged shares	....
Advances from Federal Home Loan Bank	9,794,000.00
Other borrowed money	311,000.00
Loans in process	2,301,000.00
Other liabilities	2,874,000.00
Permanent stock	....
Deferred credits	615,000.00
Specific reserves	542,000.00
General reserves	15,664,000.00
Undivided profits	5,480,000.00
Total liabilities	$332,419,000.00

Source: Annual Report, Combined Financial Statements of Members of the Federal Home Loan Bank System, 1953, Washington, D.C.

CHAPTER VII

Federal Legislation Affecting Texas Savings and Loan Associations

Federal legislation affecting savings and loan activities has been of two general types. The first has given savings and loan associations tax treatment different from that applying to other businesses. The second type—and this has occurred for the most part since 1930—has affected the method by which savings and loan associations have conducted their businesses.

Federal Tax Legislation

The first exemption from taxation obtained by the savings and loan industry was in the Wilson Tariff Act of 1894.[1] It will be recalled that the organization of the United States League of Local Building and Loan Associations was discussed in a previous chapter. One of the main functions of the League has been to serve as a lobby for the savings and loan industry, and it was largely through the efforts of the League that savings and loan associations were able to obtain special treatment in this instance.[2] The act, as finally passed, provided a 2 percent net income tax on corporations, but savings and loan associations were specifically exempted by an amendment which stated, in part, that "nothing herein contained shall apply to building and loan associations or companies which make loans only to their shareholders."[3]

The Wilson Tariff Act is of historical significance because it was the first challenge to the tax-free status of savings and loan associations, and because the savings and loan industry, through concerted action, was able to obtain preferential treatment. The victory, however, was a hollow one because the act was later declared unconstitutional, and none of the provisions were enforced.

The War Revenue Act of 1898 levied a tax on the stock and bonds of corporations, but here again savings and loan associations were given preferential treatment by a section which provided:

[1] H. Morton Bodfish (ed.), *History of Building and Loan in the United States* (Chicago: United States Building and Loan League, 1931), p. 186.
[2] "Victory in Sight," *Financial Review and American Building Association News,* 13:131, June 1894.
[3] 28 *Stat.* 556 (1895).

. . . that stock and bonds issued by co-operative building and loan associations whose capital stock does not exceed ten thousand dollars, and building and loan associations or companies that make loans only to their shareholders, shall be exempt from the tax herein provided.[4]

The Corporation Excise Act of 1909, popularly called the Payne-Aldrich Tariff Act, was an attempt to reach corporate incomes without violating the constitutional provision that no direct taxes may be levied by the federal government except by apportionment among states on the basis of population. As such, the 1909 act levied a franchise tax to be paid by corporations for the right of exercising their franchises, but the base for the tax was to be the income of the corporation. While this may seem a fairly obvious subterfuge, the constitutionality of the act was later upheld by the Supreme Court of the United States in the case of *Flint* vs. *Tracey Company*.[5]

The 1909 act is an important one in tax history as it is regarded by some as the prototype of the corporate income tax in the United States.[6] While there had been other income taxes, they were proposed as emergency legislation and were not intended to be permanent. This act, as finally passed, gave exemption to "domestic building and loan associations, organized and operated exclusively for the mutual benefit of their members."[7]

The wording of the exempting provision above would seem to indicate quite clearly that the intent of Congress was to exempt only the truly cooperative or mutual savings and loan associations from taxation. Then as today, many savings and loan associations were not mutual as to either voting rights or distribution of profits, the two usually accepted tests of mutuality.[8] Many nonmutual savings and loan associations contested the act and generally were excused from paying the tax.[9] Those that had paid were allowed a refund.

The modern income tax in the United States had its inception in the Sixteenth Amendment, ratified in 1913, which made possible the constitutional levy of an income tax without apportionment according to population among the states. Congress immediately passed the Revenue Act of 1913, which levied an income tax on corporations and individuals. Savings and loan associations were given special treatment, in that the act provided that it would not apply to "domestic building and loan associations."[10]

[4] 30 *Stat.* 455 (1897).

[5] Joseph William Tryanowski, *Exemption of Building and Loan Associations from Payment of Federal Income Tax*, (M.B.A. Thesis, The University of Texas, Austin, 1930), p. 17.

[6] *Ibid.*

[7] 36 *Stat.* 113 (1911).

[8] The two main distinguishing features of a cooperative are: (1) Voting rights—one vote per member regardless of the number of shares held, and (2) distribution of earnings—on the basis of patronage rather than ownership of stock.

[9] Tryanowski, *op. cit.*, pp. 18–19.

[10] 38 *Stat.* 172 (1915).

It is interesting to note that the qualifying phrase, "operated exclusively for the mutual benefit of their members," was omitted in the excepting proviso of the 1913 act. Granting tax relief to all savings and loan associations raises an important question of principle. Are savings and loan associations given tax relief because they are mutual organizations, or is it because of some other reason, such as their role in stimulating home ownership? It is a question that largely remains unsettled today. Savings and loan associations are elusive organizations and sometimes seem to defy classification; they have many of the aspects of mutual organizations.

In 1914 Congress passed the Emergency Revenue Law,[11] which levied a stamp tax upon the securities issued by corporations. The 1914 act specifically exempted savings and loan associations by the following proviso:

. . . provided further, that stock and bonds issued by cooperative building and loan associations . . . and building and loan associations or companies that make loans only to their shareholders, shall be exempt from the tax herein provided.[12]

While the 1913 act extended the exemption to all building and loan associations, the wording of the 1914 act employed language which would seem to exempt only cooperative associations. In all probability, this does not represent a wavering or changing attitude on the part of Congress, merely an oversight or a poor choice of words. The savings and loan representatives who appeared before congressional committees had been "assured that there would be no change in their status."[13]

The Internal Revenue Commissioner, however, ruled that nonmutual savings and loan associations were not exempt, and his ruling was upheld by the Attorney General. Some savings and loan associations were liable for the tax until it was repealed two years later by the Revenue Act of 1916.

The Revenue Act of 1916, which imposed a 2 percent tax on corporations, joint stock companies or associations, and insurance companies, provided that there should not be taxable any income received by any domestic building and loan association and cooperative banks without capital stock organized and operated for mutual purposes and without profit.

Two revenue acts were passed in 1917: The excess profits tax, and the Revenue Act of 1917. Both acts contained the following provision exempting savings and loan associations:

Corporations exempt from tax under the provisions of Section eleven, Title II of the act approved September eight, nineteen hundred and sixteen, [The Revenue Act of 1916 referred to above] and partnerships carrying on or doing the same business, shall be exempt from the provisions of this title.[14]

[11] *Ibid.*, p. 757.
[12] *Ibid.*
[13] Bodfish, *op. cit.*, p. 192.
[14] 39 *Stat.* 1001 (1917).

The Revenue Act of 1918 contained the same exempting proviso as the Revenue Act of 1916 discussed above:

Domestic building and loan associations and co-operative banks without capital stock organized and operated for mutual purposes and without profit.[15]

While there appears to have been no litigation concerning the 1916 act, the wording of the exempting proviso in the 1918 act, which was identical, gave rise to some questioning. There was no punctuation between "domestic building and loan associations" and "co-operative banks." Did the qualifying phrase "operated for mutual purposes and without profit" apply to only co-operative banks, or did it apply to savings and loan associations as well? In line with congressional policy both prior and subsequent to 1918, it would seem that the intent of the lawmakers was to extend the exemption unqualified to savings and loan associations and apply the qualifying phrase to the cooperative banks only. However, in the case of *Lilly Building and Loan Company* vs. *Miller*, the court ruled that the phrase "organized and operating for mutual purposes" applied to savings and loan associations.[16] The Treasury Department applied this reasoning, and some of the savings and loan associations were taxed under the Revenue Act of 1918.

The exempting proviso of the Revenue Act of 1921 represented a great departure from prior exemptions in that it exempted from taxation:

Domestic Building and Loan Associations substantially all the business of which is confined to making loans to members, and co-operative banks without capital stock organized and operated for mutual purposes and without profits.[17]

and further provided that gross income to an individual should not include:

So much of the amount received by an individual after December 31, 1921, and before January 1, 1927, as dividends or interest from building and loan associations, operated exclusively for the purpose of making loans to members as does not exceed $300.[18]

The 1921 act had the effect of clearing up the ambiguity of the former laws by specifically exempting building and loan associations from taxation without the requirement that they be mutual organizations. The requirement that substantially all business be conducted with members was not a severe one inasmuch as during this period a purchase of stock was usually required before a loan would be made. The $300 exemption of income from a savings and loan association was an extra bonus, which was achieved largely through

[15] *Ibid.*
[16] Tyranowski, *op. cit.*, p. 22.
[17] 42 *Stat.* 253 (1921).
[18] *Ibid.*, p. 239.

the efforts of the legislative committee of the United States League.[19] It is probably better if friends of the savings and loan industry make no attempt to justify this exemption and merely accept it as one of the advantages accruing to the industry. While the wording of the exemption was not clear, Congress apparently intended to provide an annual exemption of $300 rather than a total exemption of $300 from December 31, 1922, to January 1, 1927. The Treasury Department concurred with this viewpoint and allowed an annual deduction of $300.[20]

In substance, the Revenue Act of 1921 may properly be claimed as a victory, a substantial one, for the savings and loan industry. The exemption from corporate income taxation was broad enough to embrace virtually the entire industry, and the personal exemption placed investments in a savings and loan association on the same tax level as many government bonds. Finally, the 1921 act set the tax picture, so far as savings and loan associations were concerned, for many years to come.

The revenue acts of 1924 and 1926 made no changes in the exempting proviso applying to savings and loan associations, but the 1926 act removed the time limit, which was to expire on January 1, 1927, thereby making permanent the proviso which allowed individuals to exempt $300 of savings and loan dividends from gross income.[21]

The revenue acts of 1928 and 1932 left the exempting proviso unaltered, but the 1932 act removed the $300 personal exemption, first provided for in the Revenue Act of 1921.[22]

The Revenue Act of 1934 made no change in the exempt status of savings and loans, but for the first time it provided for exempt corporations under the now-famous Section 101. Section 101 employed the same language that had been used in the past:

Domestic building and loan associations substantially all the business of which is confided to making loans to members; and cooperative banks without capital stock organized and operated for mutual purposes and without profit.[23]

The portion of Section 101 which related to savings and loan associations remained unchanged from its first appearance in 1934 until 1951. However, beginning in 1942, savings and loan associations, along with other tax exempt corporations, were required to submit information returns. At this time, the federal government was engaged in the prosecution of a costly war and

[19] Bodfish, op. cit., pp. 199–202.
[20] Tyranowski, op. cit., p. 25.
[21] Ibid., p. 26.
[22] Savings and Loan Annals, 1932 (Chicago: United States Savings and Loan League, 1932), pp. 643–644.
[23] 48 Stat. 700 (1934).

had raised tax rates accordingly. Taxes reached such a height that the tax savings to savings and loan associations was substantial. This caused resentment on the part of tax-paying corporations, mainly those in a competitive field, such as commercial banking or other real estate lending. The House Ways and Means Committee, in an effort to make the tax burden as equitable as possible, attempted an investigation of the corporations exempt under Section 101, but there was no information available—the exempt corporations had not been filing returns. Hence, the committee made the following report, which goes quite deeply into the reasons for the recommendation, which later became law, that exempt corporations be required to file information returns:

Under existing law a large group of corporations enjoy tax exemption and many of which are not required to file information returns.

It has come to the attention of your committee that many of these exempt corporations and organizations are directly competing with companies required to pay income taxes, and that this practice is becoming more widespread and affording a loophole for tax evasion and avoidance.

These organizations were originally given this tax exemption on the theory that they were not operated for profit, and that none of their proceeds inured to the benefit of shareholders. However, many of these organizations are now engaged in operations of apartment houses, office buildings, and other businesses which directly compete with individuals and corporations required to pay taxes on income derived from like operations. Your committee was without sufficient data to act intelligently, since many of these corporations and organizations are not now required to file reports, and in the absence of such information it was felt best to continue the present tax exemption, but to require them to file reports stating specifically the items of gross income, receipts, and disbursements and such other information, and keep such records as the Commissioner of Internal Revenue may prescribe.

These returns, under the bill, are required to be made for the taxable years beginning after December 31, 1942, and all subsequent years, and it is the intent of your committee to make a thorough study of the information contained in such returns with the view to closing this existing loophole and requiring the payment of tax, and the protection of legitimate companies against this unfair competitive situation. Your committee exempted from this requirement to file returns, religious, educational, and charitable organizations which meet the definite standards set forth under Section 112 of the bill.[24]

As might be expected, the League did not take kindly to the new requirement, but at this time the tax position of savings and loan associations— they were still exempt—was by no means impregnable. In its annual report the League's Federal Legislative Committee stated:

[24] *Savings and Loan Annals, 1943* (Chicago: United States Savings and Loan League, 1943), p. 285.

The committee has also been in touch with other groups exempt under 101, farm cooperatives, labor unions, and mutual savings banks, and is of the opinion that should these groups decide to ask the Senate Committee or the Senate itself that they not be required to file returns as proposed in the House bill, it may be feasible and advisable for us to join with them. Unless some such joint move is made, however, it does not seem the course of wisdom to your committee to call attention to our own status and to seem to block or resist the quest of the Government for information.

Incidentally, it is worth noting, we think, that one of the recommendations of the Minority Members of the Ways and Means Committee in their separate report on the bill (who, it should be kept in mind, could become the Majority by action of the electorate next Fall) is that there should be a thorough overhauling of our tax system. This the Minority Report terms "one of our most pressing national problems," especially if, in the postwar era, "we are to realize maximum revenues consistent with the greatest encouragement to business and individual enterprise." The same need for a thorough overhauling of the whole tax structure has been urged for years by a number of influential Administration leaders, notably Senator George, Chairman of the Finance Committee. If such a study is undertaken with either party in power undoubtedly all present exemptions would be closely scrutinized.[25]

From 1942 to 1952, savings and loan associations were required to file information returns. In the postwar years, particularly, the tax-exempt status of all exempt corporations was subject to close scrutiny by congressional committees and others,[26] and the tax status of many exempt corporations was changed with the Revenue Act of 1951.

The Revenue Act of 1951 removed savings and loan associations from the list of institutions included under Section 101 (tax-exempt corporations) and made them subject to the same corporate income taxes paid by commercial banks:

(b) Building and loan associations and cooperative banks.—Section 101 (4) (relating to exemption from tax of building and loan associations and cooperative banks) is hereby amended to read as follows:

"(4) Credit unions without capital stock organized and operated for mutual purposes and without profit; and corporations or associations without capital stock organized prior to September 1, 1951, and operated for mutual purposes and without profit for the purpose of providing reserve funds for, and insurance of, shares or deposits in—

"(A) domestic building and loan associations, . . ."[27]

The act also amended the Home Owners Loan Act of 1933, which had provided tax exemption for federal savings and loan associations by the following:

[25] *Ibid.*, pp. 283–284.

[26] For a more complete discussion see: Jack W. Cashin, *The Taxation of Cooperatives* (M.A. Thesis, The University of Texas, 1950).

[27] *United States Code, Congressional and Administrative Service, Eighty-second Congress—First Session*, Vol. I (St. Paul: West Publishing Company, 1951), p. 370.

(d) Federal savings and loan associations.—Section 5 (h) of the Home Owners' Loan Act of 1933, as amended is hereby amended by striking out "date" (and inserting in lieu thereof the following: "date, and except, in the case of taxable years beginning after December 31, 1951, income, war-profits, and excess-profits taxes)."[28]

"Domestic building and loan associations," the term used by the Revenue Act of 1951, was so defined as to include all associations doing a savings and loan business:

(i) Definition of Domestic building and loan association—Section 3797 (a) (relating to definitions for the purposes of the Internal Revenue Code) is hereby amended by adding at the end thereof the following new paragraph:
(19) Domestic building and loan associations—The term "domestic building and loan association means a domestic building and loan association, a domestic savings and loan association, and a Federal savings and loan association, substantially all the business of which is confined to making loans to members."[29]

The Revenue Act of 1951 allowed savings and loan associations to build up free reserves to the amount of 12 percent of the withdrawable shares by the following provision:

(e) Bad debt reserves,—Section 23 (k) (1) (relating to deduction from gross income of bad debts) is hereby amended by adding at the end thereof the following: "In the case of . . . a domestic building and loan association . . . the reasonable addition of a reserve for bad debts shall be determined with due regard to the amount of the taxpayer's surplus or bad debt reserves existing at the close of December 31, 1951. In the case of a taxpayer described in the preceding sentence, the reasonable addition to a reserve for bad debts for any taxable year shall in no case be less than the amount determined by the taxpayer as the reasonable addition for such a year; except that the amount shall not be greater than the lesser of (A) the amount of its net income for the taxable year, computed without regard to this subsection, or (B) the amount by which 12 per centum of the total deposits or withdrawable accounts of the depositors at the close of such year exceeds the sum of its surplus, undivided profits, and reserves at the beginning of the taxable year."[30]

While the act removed savings and loan associations from the exempt list, it provided—and this is the great tax advantage that cooperative or near cooperative associations enjoy—that the following could be treated as a business expense, a deduction from gross income:

(f) dividends paid by banking corporations,—"(1) in the case of . . . domestic building and loan associations, amounts paid to, or credited to the accounts of, depositors or holders of accounts as dividends on their deposits or withdrawable

[28] *Ibid.*
[29] *Ibid.*, pp. 370–371.
[30] *Ibid.*, p. 370.

accounts, if such amounts paid or credited are withdrawable on demand subject only to customary notice of intention to withdraw."[31]

The Internal Revenue Code of 1954, which greatly altered many sections, did not change the tax treatment of savings and loan associations. It is oftentimes heard that state savings and loan associations are subject to income tax, while the federal associations are not. Reference to the above quotations will show that there is no difference in the treatment of the two. The tax laws allow that dividends paid on withdrawable shares may be treated as a business expense, and federal associations have only withdrawable shares. State associations may, but do not necessarily, have permanent shares; dividends paid on permanent shares are not a deduction for income tax purposes. For that reason, a profitable state association may possibly pay a corporate income tax, while a federal association of comparable size may not.[32]

To summarize the present tax treatment of savings and loan associations, they are now subject to corporate income taxes, and the only advantage they enjoy is that the dividends paid on withdrawable shares may be treated essentially the same as interest expense. Savings and loan associations are still exempt from excess profits taxes.

Federal Nontax Legislation

There have been, especially in the last twenty-five years, many acts that have affected housing and hence have affected the savings and loan industry. This section will deal, however, only with those acts that have had a close effect upon the industry in Texas. Such legislation as the Federal Reserve Acts, the National Banking Acts, price control acts, etc., while affecting the savings and loan industry, does not deal with the savings and loan industry directly and hence will not be discussed here.

The first, and in many respects the most important, piece of federal legislation which has had an effect upon the operations of savings and loan associations in Texas, was the Federal Home Loan Bank Act passed on July 22, 1932, which provided that:

As soon as practicable the board shall divide the continental United States, Puerto Rico, the Virgin Islands, and the Territories of Alaska and Hawaii into not less than eight nor more than twelve districts. Such districts shall be apportioned with due regard to the convenience and customary course of business of the institutions eligible to and likely to subscribe for stock of a Federal Home Loan Bank to be formed under this Act, but no such district shall contain a fractional part of any State. The districts thus created may be readjusted and new districts may from time to time be created by the board, not to exceed twelve in all. Such districts shall be known as Federal Home Loan Bank districts and may

[31] *Ibid.*
[32] 68A *Stat.* 205 (1954).

be designated by number. As soon as practicable the board shall establish, in each district, a Federal Home Loan Bank at such city as may be designated by the board. Its title shall include the name of the city at which it is established.[33]

Eventually the country was divided into twelve districts (later reduced to eleven), and the Home Loan Banks began operations. Texas is a part of the ninth district, which also includes Arkansas, Mississippi, Louisiana, and New Mexico and is served by the Federal Home Loan Bank of Little Rock.

The system is under the direction of the Home Loan Bank Board, which was authorized by the following provision:

For the purposes of this Act there shall be a board, to be known as the "Federal Home Loan Bank Board," which shall consist of five citizens of the United States appointed by the President of the United States, by and with the advice and consent of the Senate. Not more than three members of the board shall be members of the same political party.[34]

Under the President's Third Reorganization Plan, which became effective in 1947, the Board was made a part of the Housing and Home Finance Agency, and the number of board members was reduced to three. In August 1955 the Federal Home Loan Bank Board was removed from the Housing and Home Finance Agency and again given independent status.

In 1950 Congress passed Public Law 576, which contained provisions designed to strengthen, chiefly through influencing liquidity positions, the savings and loan industry. It required that institutions which were members of the Home Loan Bank System maintain a minimum liquidity by the following:

. . . No member of a Federal Home Loan Bank shall make or purchase any loan at any time when its cash and obligations of the United States are not equal to such amount as the Home Loan Bank Board shall by regulations prescribe: *Provided,* That such amount shall not be less than 4 per centum or more than 8 per centum of the obligation of the member on withdrawable accounts or in the case of any member insurance company, such other base as the Board may determine to be comparable.[35]

From the above quotation, it can be seen that in addition to influencing the liquidity of Texas member savings and loan associations the act may also have the effect of encouraging the institutions to hold more government bonds. It is because of this possible effect that the act has been subjected to some criticism; it appears to some to be a device to force savings and loan associations to hold government securities.

The act also made provision for member purchases of stock in the Home

[33] 47 *Stat.* 726 (1933).
[34] *Ibid.,* p. 737.
[35] 64 *Stat.* 257 (1952).

Loan Bank and a more rapid retirement of the government investment in the Federal Home Loan Bank by requiring that:

(1) Within one year after the enactment of this subsection, each member of each Federal Home Loan Bank shall acquire and hold and thereafter maintain its stock holding in an amount equal to at least 2 per centum of the aggregate of the unpaid principal of such member's home mortgage loans, home-purchase contracts, and similar obligations, but not less than $500. Such stock in excess of the amount hereby required may be purchased from time to time by members and may be retired from time to time as heretofore. One year after the enactment of this subsection, each Federal Home Loan Bank shall retire and pay off at par an amount of its stock held by the Secretary of the Treasury equivalent to the amount of its stock held by its members in excess of the amount required to be held by them by the first two sentences of subsection (c) of this section immediately prior to the enactment of this subsection and annually thereafter each Federal Home Loan Bank shall retire an amount of such Government stock equivalent to 50 per centum of the net increase of its stock held by members since the last previous retirement: *Provided,* That none of such Government capital shall at any time be retired so as to reduce the aggregate capital stock, reserves, surplus, and undivided profits of the Federal Home Loan Banks to less than $200,000,000.[36]

In order to insure further the liquidity of the savings and loan industry by providing funds to the Home Loan Banks which could be used in making advances to member institutions for the purpose of meeting withdrawals or making loans, the Secretary of the Treasury was authorized to purchase obligations of the Home Loan Banks in amounts up to $1 billion.[37]

The Home Owners Loan Act of 1933 included three points that have greatly affected savings and loan associations in Texas. Originally the Home Loan Banks were given the power to make direct loans to home owners. The 1933 act repealed this section[38] but, in its place, created the Home Owners Loan Corporation to come to the aid of distressed property owners. The Home Owners Loan Corporation was authorized to:

For a period of three years after the date of enactment of this Act, (1) to acquire in exchange for bonds issued by it, home mortgages and other obligations and liens secured by real estate (including the interest of a vendor under a purchase-money mortgage or contract) recorded or filed in the proper office or executed prior to the date of the enactment of this Act, and (2) in connection with any such exchange, to make advances in cash to exceed in the aggregate $200,000,000. Such stock shall be subscribed for by the Secretary of the Treasury on behalf of the United States, and payments for such subscriptions shall be subject to call in whole or in part by the Board and shall be made at such time or times as the Secretary of the Treasury deems advisable. The Corporation shall issue to the

[36] *Ibid.*
[37] *Fourth Annual Report, Housing and Home Finance Agency, 1951* (Washington, D.C.: United States Government Printing Office, 1951), p. 141.
[38] 48 *Stat.* 129 (1934).

Secretary of the Treasury receipts for payments by him for or on account of such stock.[39]

The Home Owners Loan Corporation accepted mortgages for a period of three years and was finally liquidated at the close of 1951 with a profit of approximately $14 million.[40]

The Home Owners Loan Act also provided for a system of federally chartered savings and loan associations:

(a) In order to provide local mutual thrift institutions in which people may invest their funds and in order to provide for the financing of homes, the Board is authorized, under such rules and regulations as it may prescribe, to provide for the organization, incorporation, examination, operation, and regulation of associations to be known as "Federal Savings and Loan Associations," and to issue charters therefor, giving primary consideration to the best practices of local mutual thrift and home-financing institutions in the United States.

(b) Such associations shall raise their capital only in the form of payments on such shares as are authorized in their charter, which shares may be retired as is therein provided. No deposits shall be issued except for such borrowed money as may be authorized by regulations of the Board.

(c) Such associations shall lend their funds only on the security of their shares or on the security of first liens upon homes or combination of homes and business property within fifty miles of their home office: *Provided,* That not more than $20,000 shall be loaned on the security of a first lien upon any one such property; except that not exceeding 15 per centum of the assets of such association may be loaned on other improved real estate without regard to said $20,000 limitation, and without regard to said fifty-mile limit, but secured by first lien thereon: *And provided further,* That any portion of the assets of such associations may be invested in obligations of the United States or the stock or bonds of a Federal Home Loan Bank.

(d) The Board shall have full power to provide in the rules and regulations herein authorized for the reorganization, consolidation, merger, or liquidation of such associations, including the power to appoint a conservator or a receiver to take charge of the affairs of any such association, and to require an equitable readjustment of the capital structure of the same; and to release any such association from such control and permit its further operation.

(f) Each such association, upon its incorporation, shall become automatically a member of the Federal Home Loan Bank of the district in which it is located, or if convenience shall require and the Board approve, shall become a member of a Federal Home Loan Bank of an adjoining district. Such associations shall qualify for such membership in the manner provided in the Federal Home Loan Bank Act with respect to other members.[41]

The act made provisions for conversion of existing institutions into

[39] *Ibid.,* p. 130.

[40] *Fifth Annual Report, Housing and Home Finance Agency, 1952* (Washington, D.C.: United States Government Printing Office, 1952), p. 135.

[41] 48 *Stat.* 132 (1934).

federal savings and loan associations, but this particular section was rather vague and was amended in 1934 to provide:

(i) Any member of a Federal Home Loan Bank may convert itself into a Federal savings and loan association under this Act upon a vote of 51 per centum or more of the votes cast at a legal meeting called to consider such action; but such conversion shall be subject to such rules and regulations as the Board may prescribe, and thereafter the converted association shall be entitled to all the benefits of this section and shall be subject to examination and regulation to the same extent as other associations incorporated pursuant to this Act.[42]

While the above amendment made it possible for many types of businesses to become federal savings and loan associations, its main purpose was to allow state-chartered associations to convert into federals. During the 1930's the Home Loan Bank System was actively working to expand the federal savings and loan program, both through organization of new associations and conversion of state institutions. Activity under this provision in Texas was discussed in Chapter V.

The National Housing Act, passed on June 27, 1934, contained many provisions which have affected Texas savings and loan associations. The main points contained in this act are the creation of the Federal Housing Administration, with the accompanying insurance programs, and the organization of the Federal Savings and Loan Insurance Corporation.

Section I provides that:

The President is authorized to create a Federal Housing Administration, all of the powers of which shall be exercised by a Federal Housing Administrator (hereinafter referred to as the "Administrator"), who shall be appointed by the President, by and with the advice and consent of the Senate, shall hold office for a term of four years, and shall receive compensation at the rate of $10,000 per annum.[43]

Section II describes the types of institutions which may obtain insurance for repair and improvement loans, as well as the types of loans which may be insured:

The Administrator is authorized and empowered, upon such terms and conditions as he may prescribe, to insure banks, trust companies, personal finance companies, mortgage companies, building and loan associations installment lending companies, and other credit insurance, against losses which they may sustain as a result of loans and advances of credit, and purchases of obligations representing loans and advances of credit, made by them subsequent to the date of enactment of this Act and prior to January 1, 1936, or such earlier date as the President may fix by proclamation, for the purpose of financing alterations, repairs, and improvements upon real property. In no case shall the insurance granted by the Administrator under this section to any such financial institution

[42] *Ibid.*, p. 646.
[43] *Ibid.*, p. 1246.

exceed 20 per centum of the total amount of the loans, advances of credit, and purchases made by such financial institution for such purpose; and the total liability incurred by the Administrator for such insurance shall in no case exceed in the aggregate $200,000,000. No insurance shall be granted under this section to any such financial institution with respect to any obligation representing any such loan, advance of credit, or purchase by it the face amount of which exceeds $2,000; nor unless the obligation bears such interest, has such maturity, and contains such other terms, conditions, and restrictions, as the Administrator shall prescribe.[44]

The provisions discussed above were amended almost immediately and have been amended numerous times since, but the amendments have been for the purpose of extending the time and expanding the program. They do not greatly alter the program; they merely enlarge upon it.

Mortgage insurance was also provided for under Title 2 of the act. To carry out the program, the Mutual Mortgage Insurance Fund, which was originally financed by a grant from the government, was established.[45] The Administrator of the Federal Housing Administration was authorized to:

. . . insure as hereinafter provided any mortgage offered to him within one year from the date of its execution which is eligible for insurance as hereinafter provided, and, upon such insuring of such mortgages prior to their date of execution or disbursement thereon: . . .[46]

The requirements for eligibility have varied from time to time with changing objectives of the Federal Housing Administraton. For the most part, the eligibility requirements include such factors as cost, maturity, interest rates, and down payments.

With the exception of the Title I repair and improvement loans, the insurance premium is paid by the lender. The Administrator is given the power to establish the rate:

The Administrator is authorized to fix a premium charge for the insurance of mortgages under this section (to be determined in accordance with the risk involved) which in no case shall be less than one-half of 1 per centum nor more than 1 per centum per annum of the original face value of the mortgage, and which shall be payable annually in advance by the mortgagee. If the Administrator finds upon the presentation of a mortgage for insurance and the tender of the initial premium charge that the mortgage complies with the provisions of this section, such mortgage, may be accepted for insurance by endorsement or otherwise as the Administrator may prescribe; but no mortgage shall be accepted for insurance under this section unless the Administrator finds that the project with respect to which the mortgage is executed is economically sound.[47]

The rate referred to above is at the present time set at one-half of one percent, the lowest allowed by the act.

[44] *Ibid.*, pp. 1246–1247.
[45] *Ibid.*, p. 1248.
[46] *Ibid.*
[47] *Ibid.*, pp. 1248–1249.

In the event of foreclosure, the lender may surrender the mortgage to the Federal Housing Administration and receive debentures in return. The National Housing Act made provisions for the type of debenture to be used, but that portion of the act was amended in 1938:

All such debentures shall be dated as of the date foreclosure proceedings were instituted, or the property was otherwise acquired by the mortgagee after default, and shall bear interest from such date at a rate determined by the Administrator, with the approval of the Secretary of the Treasury, at the time the mortgage was offered for insurance, but not to exceed 3 per centum per annum.[48]

The debentures are the liability of the Mutual Mortgage Insurance Fund, but are fully and completely backed by the United States[49] and have a maturity date two years beyond the maturity date of the mortgage for which they were exchanged.

The insurance program was expanded from time to time until it included provisions for all the following types of insurance:

Title I

Section 2 of Title I of the Act authorizes the FHA to insure qualified lending institutions against loss on loans made to finance the alteration, repair, improvement, or conversion of existing structures, and the building of small new nonresidential structures. Under the present law, this insurance is applicable to loans made on or before June 30, 1955 [subsequently extended].

Section 8 of Title I, added to the Act in 1950, authorizes the insurance of mortgages on new single-family dwellings for families of low and moderate income, particularly in suburban and outlying areas. No expiration date has been established for this program.

Title II

Section 203 of Title II authorizes the insurance of mortgages on new and existing 1- to 4-family dwellings. The principal activity of the FHA over its 18½ years of operation has been carried on under this section.

Section 207 of Title II authorizes the insurance of mortgages, including construction advances, on rental housing projects. Mortgages on projects of 12 or more units are insured.

Section 213, added to Title II in 1950, authorizes the insurance of mortgages on cooperative housing projects. Mortgages on projects of 12 or more units are insured. In a sales-type project (one built by a nonprofit corporation or trust organized for the purpose of building homes for members), the individual homes may be released from the blanket mortgage on the project and individual mortgages on these homes may be insured under Section 213. This section also authorizes the FHA to furnish technical advice and assistance in the organization of the cooperatives and in the planning, development, construction, and operation of their housing projects.

[48] 52 *Stat.* 13 (1939).
[49] *Ibid.*, p. 14.

Title VI

Sections 603 and 608 of Title VI were enacted in 1941 and 1942, respectively, to aid the production of war housing through mortgage insurance provisions somewhat more liberal than those under Sections 203 and 207. Section 603 provided for the insurance of mortgages on 1- to 4-family homes and Section 608 for mortgage insurance on rental projects. These sections became inactive after the war ended, but were revived in 1946 as part of the Veterans' Emergency Housing Program. The authority to issue commitments of mortgage insurance on new construction under Section 603 expired April 30, 1948, and new-construction commitments under Section 608 were limited to those for which applications were received on or before March 1, 1950.

Section 609 of Title VI, added in 1947, authorizes the insurance of short-term loans to finance the manufacture of housing, and the insurance of lending institutions against loss on notes given in part payment by purchasers of manufactured housing financed with insured loans.

Section 610 of Title VI, added in 1947, authorizes the insurance under Sections 603 and 608 of mortgages on specified types of permanent housing sold by the Government.

Section 611 of Title VI, added in 1948, authorizes the insurance of mortgages, including construction advances, on projects of 25 or more new single-family dwellings. The purpose of this section is to encourage the application of site fabrication and other cost-reduction techniques to large-scale home-building operations. The individual dwellings may be released from the blanket project mortgage and individual mortgages on these dwellings may be insured under Section 611.

Title VII

Title VII, added in 1948, authorizes the insurance of a minimum amortization charge and an annual return on outstanding investments in debt-free rental projects.

Title VIII

Title VIII, added in 1949, authorizes the insurance of mortgages on rental housing built on or near military reservations for the use of civilian or military personnel of the Army, Navy, or Air Force, on certification by the Secretary of Defense, and rental housing for employees of Atomic Energy installations on certification by the Atomic Energy Commission. Commitments to insure mortgages on new construction under this title are limited to those issued on or before July 1, 1953.

Title IX

This title, added to the Act in September 1951, provides for the insurance of mortgages on housing programmed for critical defense areas by the Administrator of the Housing and Home Finance Agency. Preference of opportunity to rent or purchase must be given to eligible defense workers. Section 903 of Title IX authorizes the insurance of mortgages on 1- 2-family dwellings. Under section 908, mortgages on rental projects of 12 or more units are insured. No commitment of mortgage insurance on new construction may be made under Title IX after June 30, 1953.[50]

[50] *Sixth Annual Report Housing and Home Finance Agency* (Washington, D.C.: United States Government Printing Office, 1952), pp. 207–208.

Total FHA insured mortgage loans made in Texas from 1934 through 1954 amounted to $2,022,902,000.

The National Housing Act also provided for insurance of accounts in savings and loan associations through the creation of the Federal Savings and Loan Insurance Corporation, which was to:

... insure the accounts of institutions eligible for insurance as hereinafter provided, and shall be under the direction of a board of trustees to be composed of five members and operated by it under such bylaws, rules, and regulations as it may prescribe for carrying out the purposes of this title. The members of the Federal Home Loan Bank Board shall constitute the board of trustees of the Corporation and shall serve as such without additional compensation.[51]

It can be seen from the above that the relationship between the insurance corporation and the Home Loan Bank System is quite different from that which exists between the Federal Deposit Insurance Corporation and the Federal Reserve System, for in this instance the Federal Savings and Loan Insurance Corporation is a part of, and is administered by, the Home Loan Bank System.

The corporation had a capital stock of $100 million, which was subscribed for by the Home Owners Loan Corporation,[52] and the amount still outstanding is now held by the United States Treasury. The National Housing Act was amended in 1950 to provide for the eventual retirement of the Treasury's investment:

(h) After the effective date of this subsection the Corporation is authorized and directed to pay off and retire annually at par an amount of its capital stock equal to 50 per centum of its net income for the fiscal year. Such payments shall be made promptly after the end of each fiscal year (beginning with the first fiscal year which begins after the date of enactment of this subsection) until the entire capital stock of $100,000,000 is retired.[53]

The amendment also provided that the corporation should pay to the Treasury, in place of cumulative dividends, an amount equal to 2 percent simple interest upon the original investment ($100 million) from the time since the stock was originally issued. The amount was computed at $28,981,112, after allowance had been made for previous dividends paid to the Treasury.[54]

To pay for the insurance, each association was required to pay a premium of one-fourth of one percent of all accounts in the association.[55] The follow-

[51] 52 *Stat.* 1256 (1939).
[52] *Ibid.*
[53] 64 *Stat.* 257 (1953).
[54] *Fourth Annual Report Housing and Home Finance Agency* (Washington, D.C.: United States Government Printing Office, 1951), p. 191.
[55] 48 *Stat.* 1258 (1934).

ing year the premium was reduced to one-eighth of one percent,[56] and in an act approved in 1950 it was lowered to one-twelfth of one percent.[57]

Insurance coverage was provided for:

Sec. 405. (a) Each institution whose application for insurance under this title is approved by the Corporation shall be entitled to insurance up to the full withdrawal or repurchasable value of the accounts of each of its members and investors (including individuals, partnerships, associations, and corporations) holding withdrawable or repurchasable shares, investment certificates, or deposits, in such institution; except that no member or investor of any such institution shall be insured for an aggregate amount in excess of $5,000.[58]

This provision was amended in 1950, and the coverage was raised to $10,000 per account.[59]

As originally passed, the law provided that shareholders in insured default institutions would be paid:

... either (1) a new insured account in an insured institution not in default, in an amount equal to the insured account so transferred, or (2) at the option of the insured member, the amount of his account which is insured under this section, as follows: Not to exceed 10 per centum in cash, and 50 per centum of the remainder within one year, and the balance within three years from the date of such default, in negotiable noninterest-bearing debentures of the Corporation.[60]

The reason for not paying in cash is to be found in the nature of assets of savings and loan associations. Their assets are usually of a nonliquid type, and it would be quite difficult for the insurance corporation to liquidate them at once and make cash payments to the shareholders. However, this provision proved quite bothersome, in that it was used by competitors of savings and loan associations in an attempt to discredit their insurance program. The next year an amendment was passed which greatly increased the ability of the insurance corporation to prevent failures by providing that:

(f) In order to prevent a default in an insured institution or in order to restore an insured institution in default to normal operation as an insured institution, the Corporation is authorized, in its discretion, to make loans to, purchase the assets of, or make a contribution to, an insured institution or an insured institution in default; but no contribution shall be made to any such institution in an amount in excess of that which the Corporation finds to be reasonably necessary to save the expense of liquidating such institution.[61]

With this amendment, the Federal Savings and Loan Insurance Corporation must no longer sit idly by and allow an institution to become insolvent. In-

---

56 49 *Stat.* 298 (1936).
57 64 *Stat.* 259 (1952).
58 48 *Stat.* 1259 (1934).
59 64 *Stat.* 259 (1952).
60 48 *Stat.* 1259 (1934).
61 49 *Stat.* 299 (1936).

stead, it can, as can the Federal Deposit Insurance Corporation, take steps at an early date either to avoid a failure or to minimize losses in case of insolvency.

In 1950, legislation was passed which altered the manner in which the shareholder is paid in case of liquidation. The new law requires that he be paid either by an account in a solvent association or in cash at the option of the corporation.[62] The effect of this legislation was to place shareholders in insured associations on essentially the same basis, so far as insurance was concerned, as depositors in commercial banks. However, the wording of the law, which requires that payment be made in cash as "soon as possible," has given rise to some speculation and has prompted one observer to make the probably ridiculous comment that "as soon as possible" might be as long as fifteen years.[63] As an example of its practice, the corporation liquidated one association in 1950, the first in six years, by purchasing "all the assets of the association, enabling it to liquidate voluntarily and pay all savers in cash in full."[64]

All federal savings and loan associations must have their accounts insured by the insurance corporation, and others may. It is possible for a state savings and loan association to be a member of the central bank, the Home Loan Bank System, without having insurance on its accounts. The original act allowed an institution other than a federal savings and loan association to terminate its insurance by giving ninety days notice.[65] However, in 1950 the following amendment made termination much more difficult:

Any insured institution other than a Federal savings and loan association may terminate its status as an insured institution by written notice to the Corporation, and the Corporation, for violation by an insured institution of its duty as such may, after written notice of any such alleged violation of duty and after reasonable opportunity to be heard, by written notice to such insured institution, terminate such status. In the event of the termination of such status, insurance of its accounts to the extent that they were insured on the date of such notice, less any amounts thereafter withdrawn, repurchased, or redeemed which reduce the insured accounts of an insured member below the amount insured on the date of such notice, shall continue for a period of two years, but no investments or deposits made after the date of the notice of termination shall be insured. The Corporation shall have the right to examine such institution from time to time during the two-year period aforesaid. Such insured institution shall be obligated to pay, within thirty days after any such notice of termination, as a final insurance premium, a sum equivalent to twice the last annual insurance premium paid by it.

[62] *Fourth Annual Report Housing and Home Finance Agency* (Washington, D.C.: United States Government Printing Office, 1951), p. 190.

[63] "Across Headquarters Desk," *Savings and Loan News*, 74:60, April 1954.

[64] *Fourth Annual Report Housing and Home Finance Agency* (Washington, D.C.: United States Government Printing Office, 1951), p. 190.

[65] 48 *Stat.* 1260 (1934).

In the event of the termination of insurance of accounts as herein provided the institution which was the insured institution shall give prompt and reasonable notice to all of its insured members that it has ceased to be an insured institution and it may include in such notice the fact that insured accounts, to the extent not withdrawn, repurchased, or redeemed, remain insured for two years from the date of such termination, but it shall not further represent itself in any manner as an insured institution. In the event of failure to give the notice to insured members as herein provided the Corporation is authorized to give reasonable notice.[66]

Obviously the reason for the above amendment was to give the saver in an association additional protection and to increase the likelihood of his being informed that insurance had been terminated.

The Servicemen's Readjustment Act of 1944, by providing, among other things, for the guarantee of home mortgage loans, has had a tremendous effect upon the savings and loan industry. As originally passed, the act provided that:

. . . Any person who shall have served in the active military or naval service of the United States at any time on or after September 16, 1940, and prior to the termination of the present war and who shall have been discharged or released therefrom under conditions other than dishonorable after service of ninety days or more, or by reason of an injury or disability incurred in service in line of duty, shall be eligible for the benefits of this title. . . .[67]

An amendment to the Housing Act of 1950 further extended the coverage to include:

. . . The unremarried widow of any person who met the service requirements for benefits under this title and who died, either in service or after separation from service under conditions other than dishonorable, as a result of injury or disease incurred in or aggravated by such service in line of duty (other than any such widow who by reasons of her own service is eligible for the benefits of this title), shall also be eligible for the benefits of this title; and the term "veteran" as used in this title shall include any such unremarried widow. . . .[68]

The mortgage guarantee provisions of the Servicemen's Readjustment Act were designed to assist the veteran in obtaining a home for his own occupancy and not to assist him in obtaining property for speculative or resale motives. Because of this intent, veterans were originally given one entitlement, and when that had been used they were not eligible for further use of the guarantee privilege. However, there developed many instances in which a veteran who had already used his entitlement had a real need, many times through no fault of his own, for additional assistance. In 1950 the act was amended to allow relief to a veteran in the following instances:

[66] 64 *Stat.* 259 (1952).
[67] 58 *Stat.* 291 (1945).
[68] 64 *Stat.* 74 (1952).

... In computing the aggregate amount of guaranty or insurance entitlement available to a veteran under this title, the Administrator may in his discretion exclude the initial use of the guaranty or insurance entitlement used for any loan with respect to which the security (1) has been taken (by condemnation or otherwise) by the United States, any State, or a local government agency for public use, or (2) has been destroyed by fire or other natural hazard, or (3) has been disposed of because of other compelling reasons devoid of fault on the part of the veteran: PROVIDED, That any amount paid by the Administrator under section 500 (c) of this part shall be deducted from the amount payable on the succeeding loan under that section.[69]

As originally passed, the act provided for a maximum guarantee of 50 percent of the loan or $2,000,[70] whichever was smaller, but it did allow the use of the guarantee privilege in addition to FHA insurance in the so-called "combination" loan. Later, the "combination" loan was discontinued, but any veteran who had used part of his entitlement in such a manner was allowed to obtain another loan to utilize the unused portion. In 1950, the act was amended to increase the amount of the guarantee:

(b) Any loan made under this title to a veteran who has not obviously availed himself of its benefits the proceeds of which loan are to be used for purchasing residential property or constructing a dwelling to be occupied as his home may, notwithstanding the provisions of subsection (a) of section 500 of this title relating to the percentage or aggregate amount of loan to be guaranteed, be guaranteed, if other wise made pursuant to the provisions of this title, in an amount not exceeding sixty per centum of the loan: PROVIDED, That the amount of any such guaranty shall not exceed $7,500, nor, shall the gratuity payable under subsection (c).[71]

The act has been amended many times since 1950, but the amendments have not greatly altered the working of the act as set forth above.

The National Housing Act, passed in 1934, provided for the organization of privately owned National Mortgage Associations.[72] However, the system was not a success, for:

In spite of the fact that title III [of the National Housing Act] was liberalized from time to time—to the advantage of private business and at the expense of the Federal government—private capital could never see the profit possibilities in the organization of national mortgage companies.[73]

By 1938 no private interest had chosen to operate as a National Mortgage Association, and President Roosevelt ordered the Reconstruction Finance

[69] *Ibid.*
[70] 58 *Stat.* 291 (1945).
[71] 64 *Stat.* 75 (1952).
[72] 48 *Stat.* 1252 (1934).
[73] Harry E. Hoagland, *Real Estate Principles* (New York: McGraw-Hill Book Company, 1949), p. 584.

Corporation to organize and supervise the first National Mortgage Association.

The original Federal National Mortgage Association was designed as a temporary organization to meet an emergency and was restricted in its operations to the purchase and sale of certain insured mortgages. While the Association purchased a considerable number of mortgages in its first two years of operation, its activities gradually dwindled with the cessation of construction during the war years and the abundance of financing immediately after the war. In 1948 Congress revived the Federal National Mortgage Association and greatly strengthened it by providing that it should be allowed to:

. . . (1) purchase, service, or sell any mortgages, which are insured after April 30, 1948, under section 203 or section 603 of this Act, or guaranteed under section 501, 502, or 505 (a) of the Servicemen's Readjustment Act of 1944, as amended.[74]

Extension of operations into the G. I. loan field, coupled with the tightening in the mortgage market in 1948 and subsequent years, had the effect of giving the Federal National Mortgage Association a prominent role through the next few years. Since 1948, the laws affecting the Federal National Mortgage Association have been amended from time to time without any great change having been made in its fundamental policy; it still operates as a secondary market for government insured or guaranteed mortgages.

The Housing Act of 1949 is one of the most important acts of recent years that has affected the savings and loan industry, even though it did not specifically mention the industry as such. The reason for this is that it stated, for the first time in our federal legislation, the national housing policy: "The realization as soon as feasible of the goal of a decent and a suitable living environment for every American family."[75] This goal is used as a guide—certainly it was until 1953, and it may still be today—in framing our national legislation. The choice of words in stating the goal seems to be particularly fortunate. It will be noted that the word "feasible" rather than "possible" was employed. While it may be that the wording is so indefinite it can be used to justify almost any action or lack of it, yet it does allow great emphasis on improving housing conditions without sacrificing other not less worthy goals.

The act goes on to describe the means whereby it is hoped this goal will be achieved:

The policy to be followed in attaining the national housing objective hereby established shall be: (1) private enterprise shall be encouraged to serve as large

[74] 62 *Stat.* 1207 (1949).
[75] 64 *Stat.* 413 (1952).

a part of the total need as it can; (2) governmental assistance shall be utilized where feasible to enable private enterprise to serve more of the total need; (3) appropriate local public bodies shall be encouraging and assisting the development of well-planned, integrated residential neighborhoods, the development and redevelopment of communities, and the production, at lower costs, of housing of sound standards of design, construction, livability, and size for adequate family life; (4) governmental assistance to eliminate substandard and other inadequate housing through the clearance of slums and blighted areas, to facilitate community development and redevelopment, and to provide adequate housing for urban and rural nonfarm families with income so low that they are not being decently housed in new or existing housing shall be extended to those localities which estimate their own needs and demonstrate that these needs are not being met through reliance solely upon private enterprise, and without such aid; and (5) governmental assistance for decent, safe, and sanitary farm dwellings and related facilities shall be extended where the farm owner demonstrates that he lacks sufficient resources to provide such housing on his own account and is unable to secure necessary credit for such housing from other sources on terms and conditions which he could reasonably be expected to fulfill.[76]

Of prime importance in achieving the goal is private enterprise. Government assistance is to be used for the most part to supplement and aid rather than to supplant private enterprise. However, the act did make provisions for greatly increased activity in the field of slum clearance and low rent housing. Chiefly because of these provisions, the act has been severely criticized as being "socialistic" and tending to drive private enterprise out of the real estate field.

The Housing Act of 1949 also made another important contribution to the housing field, which was to have an influence on savings and loan associations. It created the division of research, which was directed to:

Undertake and conduct a program with respect to technical research and studies concerned with the development, demonstration, and promotion of the acceptance and application of new and improved techniques, materials, and methods which will permit progressive reductions in housing construction and maintenance costs, and stimulate the increased and sustained production of housing, and [sic] concerned with housing economics and other mousing market data.[77]

Although the activities of the division of research have recently been greatly curtailed, while it was in operation it performed worthwhile service for the benefit of all real estate and related industries.

The Housing Act of 1950, while making many adjustments and amendments to prior acts, contained one provision which was both new and startling to the savings and loan industry; this was the provision for direct loans to veterans which stated:

[76] *Ibid.*
[77] *Ibid.*, p. 431.

Upon application by a veteran eligible for the benefits of this title who has not previously availed himself of his guaranty entitlement, the Administrator is authorized and directed to make, or enter into a commitment to make, the veteran a loan to finance the purchase or construction of a dwelling to be owned and occupied by him as a home, or to finance the construction or improvement of a farmhouse.[78]

This provision was subsequently used, and some direct loans to veterans were made. As might be expected, the provision was thoroughly unpopular with the savings and loan industry, although it was endorsed by the construction industry. The provision was so framed that it did not provide for direct loans unless the veteran could not get financing through private channels. Nevertheless, many considered it unfair competition on the part of the government.

In September 1950, the Defense Production Act of 1950, which provided for control of real estate credit, was passed.[79] While there had been prior instances of consumer credit control which affected repair and improvement loans made by savings and loan associations, this was the first instance of an attempt to apply a selective instrument of credit control to virtually all real estate financing. The provisions of the Defense Production Act of 1950 were the basis for Regulation X, issued by the Board of Governors of the Federal Reserve system. Regulation X governed the down payment and maturity of loans made to finance real estate. To the extent that it regulated down payments and maturity, it resembled Regulation W, which applied to consumer credit; but there the similarity ended. Regulation W was subjected to criticism because it tended to penalize the low-income purchaser—luxury-type automobiles, for example, were generally excluded from Regulation W. While a great deal of this criticism may be ignored, there was a certain element of truth in it. Regulation X went to the other extreme and applied the highest down payment requirement to higher-priced homes and applied very small down payment requirements to homes costing $7,500 or less.

[78] 64 *Stat.* 75 (1952).
[79] *Ibid.*, pp. 798–815.

CHAPTER VIII

Summary and Conclusions

In order to discuss adequately the history of savings and loan associations in Texas, it was first necessary to study the prior development in the United States, for the savings and loan industry in Texas has been influenced by changes in other parts of the country.

The Savings and Loan Movement in the United States

The first savings and loan association in the United States was the Oxford Provident Association, organized in Frankfort, Pennsylvania, in 1831.

The savings and loan movement was first thought of as a workingman's movement. To some extent this concept was justified. Savings and loan associations concentrate their lending on urban real estate, and, to a large extent, on medium- or low-priced properties. Also, the development of the savings and loan industry has accompanied industrialization and urbanization.

The savings and loan movement continued to grow in the more heavily populated areas, and by 1893 it attracted national recognition with the appearance of a report compiled under the direction of Carroll D. Wright, Commissioner of Labor. At that time, Mr. Wright found 5,860 associations, with assets of nearly $500 million.

For the most part, savings and loan associations were local institutions. However, in the latter years of the nineteenth century, "national" associations, which attempted to operate in several states, were formed. The experience of the national associations was, for the most part, unsatisfactory.

Not only have savings and loan associations increased in number and size, but there have also been changes in the methods of savings and loan operation. Most of the early associations were organized under a temporary plan which provided for dissolution at the end of a set period usually ten years.

Because of the natural inducement to continue a satisfactory and successful business, a serial plan evolved, which provided, in effect, for a series of terminating plans within one association. The serial plan permitted associations longer lives but was a cumbersome method of operation.

Gradually the serial plan gave way to a permanent plan, which permitted new members to join at any time. With the advent of permanent associations, reserve accounts came into use. In order to operate over a long period of

155

time it was necessary to retain a portion of the earnings to provide for contingencies.

Finally, the permanent stock plan, which provided that a portion of the stock could be nonwithdrawable, came into use. In effect, the permanent stock plan placed the permanent stock owners in the same position as owners of common stock in other corporations. Currently, all state savings and loan associations being organized in Texas are of the permanent-stock-plan type.

Early Development of Savings and Loan Associations in Texas

The first corporate savings and loan association in Texas was the "Young Men's Mutual Real Estate and Building Association," chartered in 1866 by a special act of the Eleventh Legislature. In one sense, the savings and loan movement did not begin in Texas until the 1880's, for it was not until then that Texas associations began assuming characteristics generally considered typical of savings and loan associations.

Texas Legislation Affecting Savings and Loan Associations

Prior to 1913, savings and loan associations were chartered by special acts of the legislature. Associations once organized were under the supervision of no state agency. This permitted abuses within the industry which many savings and loan people realized were damaging the reputation of a business which must have public confidence to flourish. Largely as a result of efforts of the savings and loan industry, the Texas legislature in 1913 passed the first law providing for general chartering and regulation of savings and loan associations. Viewed by later standards, the 1913 act, which placed savings and loan associations under the supervision of the Commissioner of Insurance and Banking, was deficient on many points. The most serious flaw in the 1913 act was that it gave the regulatory agency no control over the chartering of new associations.

In 1923 the Department of Insurance and Banking was divided into two departments, but savings and loan associations continued under the supervision of the Department of Insurance until 1929, when they were placed under the supervision of the Department of Banking.

The legislation relating to savings and loan associations passed in 1929, Senate Bill No. 111, as amended, constitutes the present legislation applicable to these associations. In many respects Senate Bill No. 111 represents a departure from the 1913 law; in general, it greatly increased the powers of supervision over state associations and has contributed toward a stronger industry. In the years since 1929, Senate Bill No. 111 has been amended repeatedly. The amendments reflect changes in the times and within the industry.

Savings and Loan Associations in Texas

The history of savings and loan activity in Texas is logically divided into five periods. The first period, from 1866 through 1915, has been discussed above. The second period, which extends from 1916 through 1929, was one of the great changes in the industry. The number of associations increased from 29 to 176 local associations. The increase in assets during this period was also spectacular. In 1916, the assets of local associations amounted to less than $2 million and those of the one foreign association to slightly over $3 million. By 1929 these figures had increased to more than $137 million and $89 million, respectively.

The next period of savings and loan activity in Texas from 1930 through 1936, was one of contraction. During this period, the number of active state-chartered associations declined from 176 to 95. The assets owned by these associations declined by $77 million or nearly 57 percent. The depression during this period caused changes in all financial industries. Probably the savings and loan industry changed more than most. The most obvious change in the industry was the failure and subsequent liquidation of many associations. In 1935 federal legislation made the first provision for federally chartered associations. By 1936, the final year of this period, there were eighty-eight federal associations; 1936 was the last year for over a decade in which there were more state associations in Texas than federals.

From 1937 through 1945 there were many changes in savings and loan operations in Texas. In 1937 there were 176 associations—87 state and 89 federal. In 1945 there were 139 associations—52 state and 89 federal. Even though the number of associations declined from 1937 to 1945, total assets of savings and loan associations in Texas increased from $83,716,000 in 1937 to $160,733,000 in 1945.

From 1946 through 1953 savings and loan activity in Texas increased greatly. In 1946 there were 139 associations, with assets of $713,409,000. In each year from 1946 through 1953 the number of state-chartered associations has increased. In 1953, the first time since 1936, the number of state-chartered associations in Texas exceeded those with federal charters.

Federal Legislation Affecting Savings and Loan Associations in Texas

Federal legislation affecting savings and loan associations has been of two types: tax legislation and nontax legislation.

Federal Tax Legislation

The first exemption from taxation obtained by savings and loan associations was granted by the Wilson Tariff Act of 1894. This law, which provided for a 2 percent net income tax on corporations, exempted savings and loan associations which made loans only to their members. However, because this act was subsequently declared unconstitutional, the advantage enjoyed by savings and loan associations was negligible. However, the Corporation Excise Act of 1909, which is regarded by many as the forerunner, if not the origin, of the corporate income tax, also exempted savings and loan associations operated "exclusively for the mutual benefit of their members." This wording would seem to imply that the intent of Congress was to exempt only the truly cooperative associations from taxation. However, the Revenue Act of 1913—the tax act passed after the ratification of the Sixteenth Amendment which permitted levying an income tax without apportionment on the basis of population—exempted all domestic savings and loan associations. While the exempting proviso wavered between exempting only the mutual and exempting all associations, for the most part the effect was to extend the exemption to all savings and loan associations.

The Revenue Act of 1921, in addition to the usual provision exempting associations from taxation, permitted shareholders an annual exemption from personal income tax of $300 in dividends received from savings and loan associations. The Revenue Act of 1934 removed the $300 personal exemption but did not make the associations themselves subject to income taxes.

With the advent of high taxes which accompanied World War II, savings and loan associations, beginning in 1942, were required to file information returns. The Revenue Act of 1951 removed savings and loan associations from the list of organizations which were exempt from taxation. However, savings and loan associations are permitted to treat dividends paid as a deduction from gross income in arriving at taxable income.[1]

Nontax Federal Legislation Affecting Texas Savings and Loan Associations

There have been, especially in the last twenty-five years, many acts which have affected housing and hence have affected savings and loan associations operating in Texas. The first legislation of this type was the Federal Home Loan Bank Act passed on July 22, 1932, which provided for a system of Home Loan Banks. Under the provisions of this act, the country was divided into twelve districts—this was later reduced to eleven—and the Home Loan

[1] As was noted in Chapter 7, the 1954 Internal Revenue Code did not alter the tax treatment of savings and loan associations.

Banks began operation. The laws relating to these banks have been amended repeatedly but without altering the main functions of the system: to provide a lender of last resort for member institutions, to provide a degree of mobility in real estate credit, and thereby to strengthen the member institutions.

The Home Owners Loan Corporation was created in 1933 to make loans to distressed property owners. The Corporation made loans for a period of three years and was finally liquidated in 1951 with a profit of approximately $14 million.

The Home Owners Loan Act, referred to above, also made provision for a system of federally chartered savings and loan associations and for conversion of state associations into federals. These provisions were particularly important during the depression years in Texas when many new federal associations were chartered and when there were also several conversions from existing state associations. However, at the present time the proportion of total associations in the state made up of federal associations is declining.

The National Housing Act of 1934 contained many provisions affecting Texas savings and loan associations, but the most important were those relating to insurance of mortgages and the creation of the Federal Savings and Loan insurance corporation. Most activity among Texas savings and loan associations in the field of insured mortgages has occurred under Title two, Section 203, which provides for insurance of mortgages on one- to four-family dwellings, and Title one, which provides for repair and improvement loans.

Insurance provided by the Federal Savings and Loan Insurance Corporation is essentially the same as that provided by the Federal Deposit Insurance Corporation. Originally, the Federal Savings and Loan Insurance Corporation provided for a delayed manner of payment in the event of failure, but in 1950 legislation was passed which made the manner of payment essentially the same as that employed by the Federal Deposit Insurance Corporation.

The Servicemen's Readjustment Act of 1944, by providing, among other things, for the guarantee of home mortgage loans, has had a vast effect upon Texas savings and loan associations. In the years since the war, Texas savings and loan associations have financed a large number of home purchases under this plan. Originally, loans made under the Readjustment Act were made by local lenders, often savings and loan associations. But in 1950 an amendment provided that in the absence of available financing, the Veterans Administration could make direct loans to veterans. This provision has been used in some Texas cities.

The Defense Production Act of 1950 provided for control of real estate credit, and the provisions of this act were the bases for Regulation X, issued by the board of governors of the Federal Reserve System. In effect, Regulation X controlled the down payment and maturity of residential loans. While actual percentage requirements were changed from time to time, the general principle employed was to raise, percentagewise, the down payment as the price of the property increased.

The result of these many laws has been to increase the role played by the federal government in all real estate financing, and, because savings and loan associations constitute the bulk of membership in the Home Loan Bank System, to increase it even more in this segment of the real estate financing industry.

Conclusions

Savings and loan activity has grown rapidly in Texas, particularly in the period since 1916. As would be expected, the industry has felt the impact of economic conditions; savings and loan business increases during periods of high construction and other real estate activity. One of the main assets of a savings and loan association is its holding of real estate mortgage loans. Consequently, the soundness of the industry depends, to a large extent, upon the quality of the properties pledged as security for these loans. As a result, savings and loan associations are, and ought to be, mindful of the necessity of accurate valuation of the properties upon which loans are made.

Over the years, savings and loan associations in Texas have come increasingly to resemble commercial banks.[2] Not only is this noticeable in the ease with which accounts can be opened and closed but also in the widely accepted principle of immediate payment upon presentation of a pass book. While the nonliquid nature of savings and loan association investments and the generally higher rate paid upon investments—as compared with bank rates—would seem to justify requiring that investors give notice before withdrawal, most associations attempt immediate payment. In order to be able to meet withdrawal demands, increasing attention is paid to liquidity ratios and other control devices.

During periods of high economic activity there is pressure to organize more and more associations. While increased economic activity would seem to call for more associations, experience has demonstrated that laxity in allowing new associations to organize can cause undesirable consequences later. Accordingly, the present Savings, Building and Loan Supervisor in

---

[2] The terminology used has come to resemble that employed by banks and other financial institutions. One seldom hears the term *shares*; instead *account* is more commonly used; *repurchased* has given way to *withdrawn*; and in some associations the *members* are referred to as *customers*.

Texas is justified in enforcing rigid standards for the organization of new associations. Savings and loan associations have at last reached such a stature that they, whether the organizers wish it or not, are inexorably tied to public welfare.

Appendix

**NAME, LOCATION, AND DESCRIPTION OF TEXAS
SAVINGS AND LOAN ASSOCIATIONS, 1893**

NAME, LOCATION, AND DESCRIPTION OF TEXAS SAVINGS AND LOAN ASSOCIATIONS, 1893

Locality	Name of association	Date organized	Plan	Shareholders	Borrowers
Anderson County					
Palestine	Mechanics Building and Loan	2-19-90	Serial	236	60
Bell County					
Belton	Young Mens' Building and Loan	8-20-83	Terminating	45	15
Childress County					
Childress	Childress Building and Loan	7- 1-91	Serial	47	8
Cooke County					
Gainesville	Hesperial Building and Savings	11-12-90	Serial	125	35
Dallas County					
Dallas	Dallas Homestead and Loan	12- 6-80	Serial	194	89
Dallas	Mutual Building	10- 1-87	Serial	218	97
Dallas	Sanger Bros. Empl. Loan and Savings	3-29-86	Serial	120	51
Denton County					
Denton	Denton Building and Investment Co.	6-26-89	Terminating	75	42
Ellis County					
Ennis	Ennis Building and Loan	7- 1-88	Terminating	51	34
Waxahachie	Ellis County Building and Savings	8- 3-88	Serial	60	23
Fannin County					
Bonham	Bonham Improvement and Loan	3-25-90	Terminating	70	25
Honey Grove	Honey Grove Building and Loan	3-21-85	Serial	75	38
Galveston County					
Galveston	Galveston Building and Loan Co.	4- 1-90	Serial	363	101
Galveston	*Texas Loan and Investment Co.	11- 1-90	Serial	510	121
Grayson County					
Denison	Citizens Building and Loan	2- 2-88	Terminating	149	67
Denison	Gate City Building and Loan	11- 5-84	Terminating	137	78
Denison	North Texas Savings and Loan	4-12-88	Serial	251	110
Harris County					
Houston	Bayou City Building and Loan	4- 1-90	Serial	87	21
Houston	Mechanics Building and Loan	5- 8-87	Serial	225	36
Houston	Mutual Building and Loan	4-15-87	Permanent	331	102

Locality	Name of association	Date organized	Plan	Shareholders	Borrowers
Hopkins County					
Sulphur Springs	Sulphur Springs Building and Loan	8-13-90	Serial	114	44
Hunt County					
Commerce	Commerce Building and Loan	5- 1-90	Serial	30	18
Greenville	Greenville Building and Loan	12-14-86	Serial	71	33
Lamar County					
Paris	*National Building and Loan	10- 1-91	Serial	998	131
Paris	Paris Building and Loan	4-12-94	Serial	110	65
Parker County					
Weatherford	Mutual Building and Loan	4- 1-91	Terminating	49	13
Weatherford	Weatherford Savings and Loan	4- 1-88	Terminating	73	23
Reeves County					
Pecos	Pecos City Building and Loan	12-20-90	Terminating	37	16
Robertson County					
Hearne	Hearne Building and Loan	2-21-91	Terminating	51	7
Smith County					
Tyler	East Texas Loan and Savings	4- 1-90	Permanent	350	145
Tarrant County					
Fort Worth	Builders Loan and Savings	10-30-90	Terminating	99	42
Fort Worth	Fort Worth Building	7-10-87	Terminating	108	75
Fort Worth	Germania Building and Loan	9- 1-89	Terminating	200	50
Fort Worth	Mutual Savings and Loan Co.	9- 1-88	Terminating	98	73
Fort Worth	Printers Building and Loan	9-25-89	Terminating	52	6
Fort Worth	Railroad Mens' Savings and Loan	11-10-91	Terminating	85	10
Fort Worth	South Side Building and Loan	9- 6-90	Terminating	93	11
Fort Worth	Workingman's Building	1-10-90	Terminating	102	61
Fort Worth	Young Mens' Building and Loan	6- 1-88	Terminating	105	70
Tom Green County					
San Angelo	West Texas Building	5-28-89	Serial	115	30
Williamson County					
Taylor	Taylor Savings and Loan	6- 1-91	Terminating	130	32

* National Association.
Source: *Ninth Annual Report of the Commissioner of Labor, 1893* (Washington, D.C.: Government Printing Office, 1894), pp. 264-267.

Index

Index

Date Due

5-16-61			
	PRINTED	IN U. S. A.	